LEAP!

101 Ways to Grow Your Business

By

STEPHANIE CHANDLER

CAREER
PRESS
Franklin Lakes, NJ

LEAP! 101 WAYS TO GROW YOUR BUSINESS
EDITED BY JODI BRANDON
TYPESET BY EILEEN MUNSON
Cover design by Ty Nowicki
Printed in the U.S.A. by Courier

To order this title, please call toll-free 1-800-CAREER-1 (NJ and Canada: 201-848-0310) to order using VISA or MasterCard, or for further information on books from Career Press.

The Career Press, Inc., 3 Tice Road, PO Box 687,
Franklin Lakes, NJ 07417
www.careerpress.com

Library of Congress Cataloging-in-Publication Data
Chandler, Stephanie, 1972–
    Leap! 101 ways to grow your business / by Stephanie Chandler.
        p. cm.
    Includes index.
    ISBN 978-1-60163-079-7
        1. Small business—Management. 2. Success in business. I. Title. II. Title: Leap! one hundred and one ways to grow your business. III. Title: Leap! one hundred one ways to grow your business.

HD62.7.C4518 2009
658.4'06—dc22

2009025580

Contents

Introduction

As business owners, we want the flexibility and freedom that is supposed to come with owning our own companies, yet many of us have no idea what that looks like. Our businesses become surrogate spouses (and sometimes our real spouses suffer the consequences). We get consumed with entrepreneurial life.

To make matters worse, we keep doing the same things but expect different results. It takes change to grow a business, but change is often surrounded by fear and perceived obstacles—excuses that can stall progress.

Following are some of the primary issues I have identified from my non-scientific examination of the entrepreneurial struggle. By no means do these apply to everyone, but I suspect a lot of people can identify with one or more items on the list.

Struggling business owners:

- Feel there aren't enough hours in a day.
- Work around the clock and need balance in their lives.
- Lack the funds needed to take their businesses to the next level.
- Get overwhelmed by the decisions that need to be made and decide it's easier to not make any decisions at all.
- Allow fear to prevent them from moving forward.
- Are afraid to ask for help.
- Resist delegating because they believe they can do it better.
- Don't conduct strategic planning and therefore lack a compass to know which direction to go next.
- Are at the heart of their business. It cannot run without them.

All of these struggles got me thinking. What do successful business owners have in common? What is the true definition of success? The following is a wish list for business owners who are ready to take a *LEAP* and move to the next level. How great would your life be if all of these were true?

Successful business owners:

➤ Have a good grasp on finances.

➤ Set their own hours and work as much or as little as they want.

➤ Know how to prioritize workload.

➤ Delegate effectively.

➤ Take vacations and don't worry about the business imploding while they are gone.

➤ Take care of their families on all levels—financially, spiritually, and emotionally. They aren't wracked with guilt because they have enough time and energy to give to everyone.

➤ Take care of themselves by exercising, getting plenty of sleep, and developing healthy habits.

➤ Have systems and people in place so that they aren't the heart and soul of the business. It runs like a finely tuned engine with or without them.

➤ Invest in marketing, business tools, and solutions that help the business grow.

➤ Take calculated risks. Sometimes they fail, but more often they succeed.

➤ Never sit idle. They are constantly learning and working to improve their knowledge.

➤ Develop plans and goals for moving forward. They always have an eye on the prize.

Welcome to the Real World

If only a step-by-step recipe existed that each of us could follow to bake the perfect business. But alas, there is no secret formula that can be applied to all businesses. Just take a look at the franchise model. When a business runs like a well-tuned motor and can be replicated, that is a great sign of success. However, even with the cookie-cutter approach, there are no guarantees. A franchised sandwich shop may flourish in one neighborhood and crumble in another, even though both have identical business strategies. A recipe doesn't always work, and sometimes a cake comes out flat. But a good chef will keep tweaking the recipe until he finds the right combination.

On the following pages you will find many ingredients for growing your business. Not every ingredient is right for every business; your job is to determine which ingredients are right for your unique business recipe.

This book could have easily been titled "1,000,000,001 Ways to Grow Your Business," but I had to narrow it down to 101. Otherwise, this would read like an encyclopedia, and that wouldn't be fun for anyone. To compile the list, I started with my own experiences. Following a decade-long career in the Silicon Valley, I built a retail business (a bookstore) from the ground up and sold it several years later. I also own a publishing and marketing company and several online ventures. I have enjoyed the process of learning at every turn.

I also reached out to some of my favorite experts for advice. More than a dozen authors graciously allowed me to interview them for this book, including Jay Conrad Levinson, Seth Godin, David Meerman Scott, David Allen, Ford Harding, Elinor Stutz, Garrett Sutton, and several others.

And I couldn't have written this book without including lessons from the real world. I interviewed dozens of business owners and included many of their personal stories and insights throughout the 101 strategies. Each chapter also concludes with a profile of a business owner who successfully made the *LEAP* by taking their business to the next level. These stories inspired me, and I hope they inspire you too.

What's the Deal With *LEAP*?

There is an old saying: "Leap and the net will appear." I believe this is true—though first you must *prepare* to make that leap. You wouldn't jump out of a plane without first learning how to deploy your parachute. You shouldn't make major business decisions without first doing some research and developing a plan.

We take leaps of faith throughout our lives. We date various people before we settle on "the one." We endure jobs we hate before finding the courage to leave. We raise kids and send them off to school trusting that they will be safe and will come home happy at the end of the day. We help a friend in need. We drop money into the donation can at the checkout counter. We persevere and endure the challenges of daily life. In each of these *LEAP*s, we have the opportunity to learn from our successes, and perhaps more importantly, we can learn from our mistakes.

This book is divided into these four important parts:

Leverage (Part 1): Use your resources and form a plan to grow your company.

Execute (Part 2): Take action on your plans to move forward.

Accelerate (Part 3): Pick up the pace and cross the chasm to the next level.

Prosper (Part 4): Reap the rewards while you maintain momentum.

My hope this that you will find the ideas and ingredients you need to help you take your business to the next level and to finally enjoy the rewards of your hard work.

Are you ready to *LEAP*?

Part One

Leverage
(Build a Machine)

CHAPTER 1

"A goal without a plan is just a wish."

—Antoine de Saint-Exupery

Establish a Launch Pad

1 Get a Vision

Do you have a vision for your business? Can you picture where you want it to be in five, 10, or 20 years? If you're like most business owners, there is a good chance that you're a victim of one of the following:

> You have been too busy running your business to stop and think about the Big Picture.

> You had a vision for your company when you started, but you haven't had time to think about that in ages.

> You can't see beyond the end of the month. because you're too focused on trying to make the bills.

> Vision? What's that?

The beauty of establishing a vision for the future of your company is that it's all yours. You can make it as big or as small as you want. That's right—I said *as small* as you want. Some people don't want the added responsibility of running a large company, and there is absolutely nothing wrong with that. What's more important is that you figure that out early on because it will help shape your decisions in the long run.

Establishing your vision gives you a focal point that you can refer to whenever there are business planning considerations. If your goal is to expand into international markets, then you would probably want to put more focus into building your Web presence. If your plan is to stay local, a Web presence is still important, but how you administer that will be much different.

When considering your vision for your company, remove the potential obstacles. Your ultimate vision is the equivalent of a dream and the biggest goal you want to achieve.

If money were no object, what would your business look like? (You can figure out the money part later.) Are there new markets that you want to penetrate? Is there a service that you want to launch? Do you want to establish an international presence?

Spend some time thinking about your vision for your company. Consider the questions in the previous paragraph and how the end result would fit in to your lifestyle. Then commit your vision to paper. It might be as simple as a few sentences, or you might dig deeper and outline multiple goals and a time line for achieving them.

Athletes are known for using visualization as a tool. Michael Phelps was the U.S. team star of the 2008 Olympics and reportedly visualized winning the swimming competitions. When visualization meets preparation, anything is possible.

Create a Vision Board

A vision board is a visual representation of your goals for the future. These are typically comprised of pictures, words, and phrases clipped from magazines. You can even create multiple boards: one for business, one for family, and one for personal goals. Post your board(s) in your office or another place where you will see the images every day so you can focus on what you're working toward.

Resources

Do you need help getting a vision? If you're stuck, lack inspiration or you want to develop an entirely new outlook, here are some great books to help you find the answers.

- *The Success Principles: How to Get from Where You Are to Where You Want to Be* by Jack Canfield

- *The Passion Test: The Effortless Path to Discovering Your Life Purpose* by Janet Attwood
- *Awakening the Entrepreneur Within: How Ordinary People Can Create Extraordinary Companies* by Michael Gerber
- *The Secret* (DVD or book version)

2 Reestablish Your Priorities

Running a business is one of the toughest challenges you can choose in life. In fact, it's a lot like parenting. It places unexpected demands on your time and energy, requires nurturing and love, keeps you up at night, demands structure and discipline, teaches you valuable lessons about yourself, and, despite all of the long hours and hard work, it can be extremely rewarding.

Unfortunately, many business owners become so overwhelmed with the daily demands of running a business that they end up losing focus on the future. They want more for their business and their life, but they don't take time to figure out how to get there.

Many of the business owners that I encounter are struggling with the three Biggest Business Demands (BBDs):

- Time.
- Money.
- Effort.

I would bet that, when you started your entrepreneurial adventure, you underestimated how much time, money, and effort it would take. And odds are that you continue to struggle with BBDs on a daily basis. BBDs are the factors that lead to entrepreneur burnout and are at the heart of our excuses. Can you relate to these?

> *"I don't have time to focus on the future; I'm just trying to get through today...."*

"There aren't enough hours in a day...."

"If only I had more money...."

"If I just work harder, I'll make more money...."

"I'm so exhausted...."

"I feel guilty for not spending more time with my family...."

"It's been a slow month. I don't know if I can keep doing this. Maybe I should go get a job...."

Shifting From Overwhelmed to Overjoyed

I have personally been a victim of the BBDs. I have worked around the clock, complained about not having enough time, and gotten caught up in the self-imposed demands of running a business. Entrepreneurs tend to have Type-A personalities. We are overachievers to the 10th degree. We are perfectionists. We exhaust ourselves.

Eventually I realized that I had a choice to make: I could keep going at an insane, unhealthy pace and sacrifice time with the people who were most important in my life, or I could make some big changes.

What I learned was that building a successful business doesn't have to equate to a 60-hour work week. When I took a step back to reevaluate, I realized that I had way too many balls in the air and many of them didn't align with my goals. In fact, I was keeping myself so busy that I had lost sight of what my goals were in the first place.

Personal Priorities

No amount of success is worthwhile if you aren't personally fulfilled. Although many of us derive a certain amount of satisfaction and even self-worth from our achievements, at the end of the day, you can't hug your business. Your business can't help you celebrate a milestone birthday or laugh with you over dinner.

Jenifer Landers, a personal development coach who specializes in working with artists and creative business owners, is also a single mom who shares custody of her 10-year-old daughter. "When Stella gets home from school at 2:30, I shut everything else down," says Jenifer. "My goal is to give her my complete attention and to be fully present with her."

In the summer when school is out, Stella occasionally gets to attend meetings with her mom. "She loves it, and I love that she's learning what it's like to be independent and do your own thing," says Jenifer. "I get to teach her how to make her own choices and do what she wants with her life instead of just showing her the path to getting a job."

To make up for her shortened workday, Jenifer often returns to working on her business after Stella goes to bed. "It's completely worth it," she adds. "I just work my schedule around her and put in extra time when Stella is asleep or with her dad. I'm so grateful for our time together. I just make it work."

Try This

Do yourself a favor and make sure your personal priorities are in order. It might mean putting your spouse ahead of your monthly networking meeting. It might mean that you need to make time to find a life partner, connect with friends, or start a family. Maybe you need to define some boundaries around when you work and when you play or rediscover what it's like to have fun!

Make a detailed list of the personal priorities and boundaries you want to set in your life. Items might include any or all of the following:

> Institute a weekly date night with my spouse.

> Have dinner with my family five nights each week.

> Spend one-on-one time with each of my kids each week.

> Schedule lunch with a friend once each week.

➤ Work out three mornings each week.

➤ Sign up for a dating service.

➤ Read a novel.

➤ Get a massage.

➤ Take two vacations this year.

➤ Pick up kids early on Fridays and spend the afternoon together.

➤ Play golf once each month.

➤ Sign up for tennis lessons.

➤ Write my life story.

➤ Write a book.

➤ Stop working on weekends.

Whatever your personal priorities are, commit them to paper and develop a plan for bringing them to life. Though you will probably have to make some adjustments, I bet that you will find it far more rewarding both personally and professionally when you bring joy back into your life.

Resources

- *Slowing Down to the Speed of Life: How to Create a Simpler, More Peaceful Life from the Inside Out* by Richard Carlson and Joseph Bailey
- *The Last Lecture* by Randy Pausch

3 Make Your Own Rules

So you have your own business and by now you have probably learned from a variety of sources how it is "supposed" to be done for your industry. Maybe you attended training sessions or participated in a certification program. You've probably read books or attended trade events and have learned the "rules" for operating your type of business.

This is all great, and I am an advocate of learning new strategies from every possible source. However, just because something works for someone else, or because it's the way the majority of businesses in your industry are doing things, that doesn't necessarily mean it's the only way to do things. In fact, it may not even be the best way to do it.

For example, when the virtual assistance field became popular several years ago, most Virtual Assistants (VAs) were taught to set a low hourly rate, to bill clients based on a monthly retainer with a five- or 10-hour minimum, to give discounts for bigger retainer packages, and to bill clients for their time down to the minute.

Over time, some VAs decided to change the rules. They began selling service packages instead of hourly packages. They dropped the monthly minimums in order to attract more clients. They discovered untapped niches and raised their rates to more livable wages. They leveraged the talent of less-expensive VAs and built teams of people to do the work instead of operating as a one-person show. They changed the rules and reaped the rewards.

What rules have been laid out for you in your industry? Are you limiting your growth potential because you only offer bundled packages instead of monthly service options? Have you had ideas for your business that you dismissed because they weren't the norm for your industry?

As you read through this book you will encounter stories and ideas from businesses vastly different from yours. Consider how their strategies might work for you.

4 Join a Mastermind Group

In *The Success Principles* by Jack Canfield, Canfield says, "I don't know anybody who has been super-successful who has not participated in master-minding." Some of the greatest minds in history have leveraged a mastermind group. In Napoleon Hill's book *Think and Grow Rich,* Hill emphasized the importance of participating in a mastermind group. Though Hill wrote the book decades ago, his advice is as valid as ever. The right mastermind group is powerful tool for growing your business.

A mastermind group is typically made up of five to 10 people who meet on a regular basis to discuss business ideas and challenges. These can be conducted in a variety of ways. A group can meet weekly, monthly, quarterly, or twice each year. Meetings can be in person or over the phone. Each group has its own unique parameters that work for its members.

There are many benefits of participating in a good mastermind group, including:

➤ It's a safe place to discuss your business and receive honest feedback.

➤ You learn from what others are going through.

➤ Ideas and solutions are generated on the spot.

➤ It can be uplifting and motivating.

➤ It helps you be accountable for your progress.

➤ You learn when you have a bad idea—before you find out the hard way.

➤ You get reinforcement for great ideas with extra ideas to refine them.

➤ You can talk through your ideas and gain clarity.

➤ You build valuable relationships with people you respect.

I firmly believe that every business owner who wants to achieve growth should participate in a mastermind group. Though you can probably ask around or search the Internet and find one, it is better if you can be referred into one with people you respect, or launch your own group and hand-pick the members.

Ideally the group should consist of people from different industries, but in the same category. For example, service professionals from several industries make the perfect recipe for a group. Each should have some experience under their belt (no newbies allowed—this is a tool for growth, not teaching) and collectively the group should have a broad range of experiences. It is also essential that the group be made up of people you like, respect, and trust.

5. Know Your Niche

One of the biggest mistakes you can make is to try to be all things to all people. A target market gives you the opportunity to differentiate your company from the competition. When you identify your target market—your niche—it will give you and your business the benefit of focus.

Let's look at some big examples:

➤ **Wal-mart** is the low-price leader, catering to families that want to stretch their dollar. They aren't out to capture the high-earners, and they don't have to. There are plenty of thrifty consumers keeping them in business.

➤ **Nordstrom** is at the other end of the spectrum. This high-end department store caters to the affluent. From the sparkling décor and top-notch service to impeccable in-store displays, everything about Nordstrom appeals to its niche.

➤ **Apple's iPod** is targeted toward the young consumer. The ads are hip and edgy and clearly speak to the 15-to-25 age group. Apple hit the ball out of the park on this one because the buzz caught on. The appeal has reached across many age groups. This is the ultimate sales success strategy that every business hopes for. The lesson here is that Apple remains focused on its target audience—the rest is just gravy.

➤ **Nintendo's Wii** video gaming system was initially targeted toward the obvious audience: kids. As competition in the gaming industry has increased, Nintendo made a bold move by adding another niche to its plan: adults who exercise. By introducing Wii Fit, an interactive exercise program, the company quickly corned a new niche market. Nintendo will certainly continue developing new products for its core market of kids, but now has a new niche to develop products for. This can be an excellent growth strategy when executed properly.

Now let's look at an example from the small business world. A Web design company that offers design services "for just about anyone" may lure in some clients, but will be hard-pressed to set the business apart in a competitive situation. On the other hand, a Web design company that caters to the medical industry is going to have a significant edge in that field over competitors that are generalists.

See how this works?

Matt Cooper, VP of Strategy and Operations for Accolo, Inc., a company that provides managed recruiting services, agrees that focus is key: "When you're small and trying to stay profitable, it's easy to chase every deal that passes in front of you.... We finally zeroed in on our core: helping smaller growth companies build a function they didn't have (rather than replacing or augmenting the recruiting of larger companies. Once we focused on that market, we shifted our marketing, pricing and delivery to that one thing. Our new client acquisition rates increased while our client turnover rates decreased.... Sometimes the best thing you can do for your company is say 'no' to a deal."

To define a niche for your business, ask yourself the following questions:

➤ What do my top clients have in common? Are they in the same industry, same age range, same demographic?

➤ What do my favorite clients have in common?

➤ What kinds of people or industries could benefit from my products and/or services?

➤ What industries do I have experience in that I could leverage to gain market share?

➤ What industries or people have a problem that my products and/or services solve?

➤ What kinds of people or industries do I most enjoy working with?

Once you identify your niche, put your energy into reaching your audience. When you let the world know that you sell widgets for green companies, you are going to begin attracting green businesses that want to learn more about your widgets.

As you move forward, nearly every business decision you make should take into account your niche audience. For example, throughout your business development practices, you will want to keep questions like these in mind:

➤ Will this new service solve a problem for my audience?

➤ Can my audience afford this price point?

➤ What motivates my audience to buy?

➤ What magazines does my audience read?

➤ What Websites does my audience visit?

➤ What other businesses are already reaching my audience?

➤ How could we form strategic alliances with those companies?

Focusing on a niche can be incredibly powerful and has the potential to change the trajectory of your entire business. You may skip over many topics in this book, but this is one that I encourage every business owner to consider.

Get Uncomfortable

I have some news for you. There is no cookie-cutter approach to any business that works for everyone.

Though we can and should seek to learn from others who have achieved some level of success, there is no guarantee that what has worked for them will work for us.

Michael Port, author of *The Think Big Manifesto,* says we need to "[u]nhook from the guru trap," and I completely agree. When you expect someone else to have all of the answers, you are setting yourself up for disappointment. "We have reassigned meaning to this term 'guru,'" says Port. "You're supposed to follow someone else's 'blueprint' to fix your problems, but it doesn't work that way."

Port says that instead of following someone else's step-by-step solution, look for opportunities to learn. Perhaps more importantly, look within yourself for answers. "Great leaders are great learners," says Port. "The guru trap separates us, makes us inferior, smaller.... We must find teachers wisely."

Port is heading up a movement through his site, *www.ThinkBigRevolution.com,* and says it's all about thinking bigger: "Each person should decide what thinking big means to them. It should not be defined by others." Port wants you to get comfortable with discomfort. He says, "Our society is comfortable. When it's a little cold, you turn the heat up. When it's hot, you turn on the air conditioning.... Comfort doesn't propel people to do bigger things.... If you want to speak in public, you may be nervous. Start with five people, go out there and get comfortable with the discomfort," says Port. "Next, go speak to ten people. Keep going until you find new discomfort in 5,000 people."

Ultimately, you have to push yourself out of your comfort zone so that you can define what success and big thinking mean to you. According to Port, "You have to stand for something and let it guide you in whatever you do."

"Don't look to me to be a revolutionary; look to you," say Port. "Make a commitment [to yourself] that puts you in a place that makes you slightly uncomfortable." In a nutshell, be open to guidance from others, but check in with your gut and stretch yourself outside of your comfort zone. That's big thinking and it's key to making big things happen for your business.

Assess Your Business Image

A poor business image plagues many small businesses. Homemade flyers and inexpensive business cards scream "amateur." If your local chamber of commerce or hometown newspaper includes flyer inserts, take a close look at them. Are you going to sign up for body waxing from the aesthetician who has a black-and-white flyer that clearly looks like something she threw together herself, or are you going to call the salon with the glossy full-color flyer and compelling sales message? If you're seeking a quality service, you're going to go with the company that projects quality.

One of the easiest ways to make a small company look big is to enlist the talent of a marketing company to dress up your promotional materials. Keep in mind that, in addition to looking great, the content should be equally impressive. A good marketing consultant or copywriter can come up with the right words and a call to action that lures in customers.

Here are some other business image considerations:

➤ If you have a physical location such as an office or a storefront, how does it look? Is it clean, appealing, and easy to navigate? Enlist the help of a third party who will give you honest feedback. It might be time for a fresh coat of paint, or perhaps you need to hire a janitorial service to make sure the restrooms are always clean.

➤ Evaluate your own image. Are you presenting yourself to the world in a way that makes you proud? Though jeans may be acceptable in your field, that doesn't mean you shouldn't wear slacks. It's almost always better to be over-dressed than under-dressed.

➢ Evaluate your employees. Are they projecting the company image that you want? Maybe you need to order some polo shirts with logos on them or establish a dress code. Would you be more inclined to hire the pest control guy in a rock-and-roll t-shirt and shorts, or the one in a crisp company shirt and Dockers?

➢ Take an objective look at your Website. Does it look professional? Is the copy well written? Is it easy to navigate? Does it compel visitors to take action? We'll cover Web strategies in Chapter 10, but you can start by assessing your site and asking others to provide input.

8 Create Your Business Growth Action Plan

Coming up with ideas to grow your business is the fun part, but putting them into action is an entirely different ball game. This is also where a lot of business owners get stuck. They are either afraid to take the leap or don't know what to do next. Here's where having a plan comes in handy.

Studies show that goals that are committed to paper are more likely to be completed. As you read through this book and identify ideas for your business, make sure to write them down. Once you have a good, solid set of ideas, your next step is to prioritize them. You can't tackle them all at once, so put them in order of importance.

Finally, identify the action steps needed to complete each goal. Sometimes a goal seems so big that you don't know where to start. But when you break a goal down into small, digestible bites, you can begin to tick off the list of actions one by one.

The chart on page 27 can help you prioritize your action items.

Business Growth Action Plan				
Priority	Action Item and Related Tasks	Delegate To	Target Completion Date	Date Completed

Here is how to use each column:

Priority:

Once you list your goals, designate each with priority 1 through 4, with 1 being top priority and 4 being lowest priority.

Growth Goal and Related Action Items:

Here is where you list your goals and the required action items to complete each one. If that's too overwhelming for you, create a separate action item sheet for each goal.

Delegate To:

Learn to delegate whenever possible so that you can focus on what you do best. For every item on your list, identify who you can delegate it to.

Target Completion Date:

Set a realistic date that isn't too far out. The time is now!

Date Completed:

Does this really need clarification? Enjoy the rewards of crossing items off your list.

You can download this chart as an Excel worksheet at *www.BusinessInfoGuide.com/leap-downloads.*

 Success Interview

Ken Goodrich

24/7 Service Corporation

DBA Yes! Air Conditioning & Plumbing

www.ChooseYes.com

Year Founded:	2001
Business Partners:	Lance Fernandez, Jon Catalano
Number of Employees:	93

What does your company do?

Residential and light commercial air conditioning and plumbing service and replacement.

What led you to start your business?

24/7 Service Corporation is my second business. I built my first business Racee Air Conditioning from 1987 and sold it to a public company (ARS) in 1997.

I started Racee as most small business owners do, knowing a trade and thinking I can do it better than my boss. I can still recall the day when I was sitting in my truck in front of a vendor's office, with no money, no more credit with this vendor, and thinking I have to do this another way other than doing the work and trying to grow a company. I took out a dirty legal pad I had laying on the seat of my truck and crafted this simple plan.

1. Build a business that someone would want to buy for a large sum of money.
2. Go out and recruit the best and brightest people I could find and share my vision with them. Inspire them to sacrifice and be part of my dream.
3. Make these people part of my exit strategy so they could win, too.
4. Create business systems for everything we do so that we could deliver consistent service to our clients that would make them come back for more.
5. Everything we do will be so far ahead of the competition and our clients' expectations that we could demand a price that would ensure a profit.

Six years after that plan was created on that dirty legal pad, I sold Racee Air Conditioning for millions of dollars. Every key member of the Racee team who stuck by me got a wealth gain by that transaction as well.

In 2001, I had lived out my non-compete with the company that bought Racee, ARS, and began to hear grumblings of another consolidation within the industry within the near future. I contacted Lance Fernandez and Jon

Catalano, who were former key personnel of my former company, and told them, "We're getting the band back together."

Jon and Lance agreed to come on board and build another air conditioning company with the end in mind: build and sell. Our plan was to acquire old established air conditioning companies in Las Vegas, Nevada, and Phoenix, Arizona, make them profitable, and create another liquidity event like Racee—only bigger.

We sold 24/7 Service Corporation to ARS AGAIN for 10 times the amount of the Racee transaction February 1, 2008.

Was there a specific turning point when you realized your business was moving to the next level?

Once I felt comfortable that my key managers could handle the day-to-day operations better without me, I realized that I could work on the growth of the business.

What processes or procedures have you implemented that have helped grow your company?

1. Pricing methods that ensure profits.
2. Daily training and motivation for all team members.
3. Fifty-two-week recruiting efforts to ensure we always have the best and brightest on our team.
4. Fifty-two-week marketing plans to ensure a constant lead flow into the company.
5. Documented sales process to ensure a constant revenue stream into the company.
6. Documented client fulfillment processes to ensure a consistent, enjoyable client experience with the company.
7. Heavy staffing on inside and outside accounting to ensure proper accounting and operating statistics by which to run the business.

8. Operating budgets and key performance indicators to ensure that we plan our work and work our plan.

9. Monthly celebrations and rewards when we obtained our numbers to ensure that everybody wins.

10. The message of "we are the best at what we do" delivered to the entire team every day.

What are some of the best marketing strategies you have used to grow your company?

1. Clean, professional personnel, facilities, and equipment.

2. Hired a PR firm.

3. Billboard in front of our largest competitor for recruiting.

4. Small postcard reminders for service mailed throughout the entire city monthly.

5. Telemarketing.

6. Having each of our technicians document items of future concern on each client's invoices and reminding the client months later that we should take care of that concern.

7. Professionally created brand name and logo.

8. Hired a disabled woman to call each competitor in the phone book monthly and search for disconnected phone numbers, and have the phone company direct those numbers to our call center.

9. Acquire every bankrupt or retiring competitor that we could find and convert their clients to ours.

10. Twice a year, give an underprivileged person in the community a free air conditioning repair and have the news stations cover the event.

Are there any ways that you have leveraged the Internet to grow your business?

1. We hired an Internet marketing firm that has gotten us listed in the top three of Internet searches for our type of business.
2. We have partnered with several Internet lead generation companies that provide screened referrals to their clients for our services.
3. The Internet now represents 35 percent of our leads.

What challenges have you faced and how have you overcome them?

1. Learning that a business has very little to do with your particular trade or profession. I overcame this by finding out what the client wants to buy and doing that rather than trying to force them to buy what I wanted to sell them.
2. Learning how to lead and manage people. You have to touch a heart before asking for a hand. I overcame this by reading leadership books and by trial and error.

How do you balance your work and personal life?

My work is no longer work; it's my passion. I have structured the business so that I have more time for my personal life than the average guy and love what I do. By the way, I am sitting on my patio in Laguna Beach, California, during a one-month vacation with my family writing this for you.

If you were starting over today, what would you do differently?

1. Identify a business that had the highest potential for success and a wealth gain exit strategy within five years of its inception. Probably something I knew very little about.

2. Go out and recruit the best and brightest core team I could find that may have some knowledge about that business or just good businesspeople. I would look for a finance person, a marketing/sales person and some professional managers. Make them part of the wealth gain exit strategy so that they have something to work toward.

3. Write a business plan and, with my team, create all of the business systems necessary to operate that business profitably.

4. Acquire the necessary capital to execute the plan.

5. Create a training process and begin to recruit and hire the rest of the team and take several months to practice, drill, and rehearse until the team knew the business systems instinctively.

6. Create key performance indicators for everything we do, and track everything. Adjust as necessary.

7. Kick off the marketing, and start acquiring clients and making profits.

What advice do you have for other business owners?

Learn how to lead, manage, and motivate people and make them part of your cause; create business systems that will make your clients love doing business with your company, and never, ever, ever give up.

CHAPTER 2

*"You don't get paid for the hour. You get paid for
the value you bring to the hour."*

—Jim Rohn

Infrastructure

9 Build a Business You Can Sell

When someone buys a business, he/she is buying the *system* behind the business. The seller must provide a long list of details ranging from operations procedures and several years of financial records to sales processes and vendor lists. You can't sell a business unless the new owner can pick up where you left off and be just as successful.

Even if You Don't Ever Plan to Sell...

The majority of small businesses, especially service businesses, are in no position to be sold. When a company revolves around the talent of just one or two individuals, it would likely be a disaster if those individuals were to leave.

For example, if you own a graphic design company and do all of the design work yourself, you don't have a company to sell. You can't pick up your company and hand it to someone else, because your clients will hit the road when you leave. However, if you have a team of designers doing the work, then you are closer to having a business that can be replicated and ultimately sold.

Another big problem is when the owner is the one and only salesperson and, worse yet, those sales are built on personal relationships. If clients are giving you business because you have a great time on the golf course together, what do you think would happen if someone new stepped in to your shoes? Even the best golfer on the planet cannot be assured that the clients will have the same loyalty.

The model of being the heart of your business is a problem not only if you plan to sell, but if anything were to ever happen to you. If you get hit by a bus and get laid up for several months, can your business run without you? If something really catastrophic happened, would your business be an asset after you're gone? Or would it have to be dissolved because the legacy you left behind was that *you were the business*? Can you take a vacation and come back to a business that ran smoothly while you were gone?

Andrew Rogerson, author of several books, including *Successfully Sell Your Business: Expert Advice from a Business Broker,* says, "The Golden rule is to put your feet in the shoes of the other party. Consider how a buyer, the buyer's accountant, and a lender would view the state of your business. Each of their views would be different, but the better you build your business for each of these parties, the more easily the business could sell and the higher the purchase price."

One of the key components a potential buyer looks for in a business is its ability to generate cash. The more cash a business generates, the more leverage it will have when it comes time to sell, because cash generation typically equates to a higher selling price. Written processes and procedures are also essential to a smooth transition and a business should have important policies up to date such as employee contracts, commercial leases, and related data.

"Which business do you think is worth more? A business that makes $500,000 per year, sales are declining slightly each of the last 4 years, the current owner works 7 days per week, hasn't taken a vacation in 8 years, the lease expires in 12 months and has no right of renewal," asks Rogerson. "Or the business that makes $450,000 per year, sales have increased at 10% per annum for the last four years, the current owner works four days per week and has taken three weeks of vacation each of the last four years as well as a three month family break in one of those years?"

As you build your plan to grow your business, keep the thought of selling it in mind—even if you never plan to do that. A business should be a self-contained asset—one that functions with or without the owner. Without systems and processes, what you really have is a hobby that makes some money.

10 Develop an Organization Chart

There are seven basic functions of every business:

1. Sales.
2. Marketing.
3. Customer Service.
4. Human Resources.
5. Operations.
6. Production.
7. Accounting.

In the early stages of a small business, the owner wears many hats. An owner that is responsible for all seven basic business functions is an owner that is going to burn out quickly. The sooner you can establish an organization chart, the better.

No matter where you are in your business, the process of creating an organization chart is a valuable exercise in plotting the future. Whether you have a few of the positions filled or you're currently running all of them, putting the roles on paper can help you plot the future.

Decide what role you want to play in the long run. Do you want to be CEO? Do you want to be head of marketing? Where are your strengths and where are your weaknesses? What responsibilities can you delegate to an employee, contractor, or service provider? For example, do you have a bookkeeper or a CPA handling your finances? If not, get one. It will free up your time to focus on what you do best, and it may come with some hidden benefits.

As you go through this exercise, consider the priorities for acquiring talent. Is marketing your weakness? Then hiring someone to do this should be a priority. Would your customers benefit from better customer service? Then build that into your long-term plan. What would your customer service organization look like?

Resource

You can download a free modifiable organization chart template from Microsoft: *office.microsoft.com/en-us/templates/TC060889761033.aspx.*

11 Hire a Virtual Assistant

One of the most wonderful industries to emerge in recent years is the growing field of virtual assistance. A Virtual Assistant (VA) is someone who provides business support remotely, usually from a home office. VAs have a wide variety of skills, ranging from basic administrative functions like typing letters and entering contacts into a database to more advanced skills such as Internet marketing support and telemarketing.

Costs for these services depend on where the VA is located, how much experience she has, and her skill level. I personally use the services of several VAs. Each has her own unique skill set and handles a different set of tasks for me. Not one of them lives in my hometown. In fact, I have worked with several in entirely different states. The Internet makes it incredibly easy to conduct business from just about anywhere.

Stacy Karacostas, owner of SuccessStream, a marketing coaching business in Seattle, Washington, says, "Hiring a team of Virtual Assistants has been the single best strategy I've used to make more and work less.... When my part-time in-house employee quit a couple years ago, I bit the bullet and hired a VA for myself. Now they handle all my online marketing and business tasks, including running my shopping cart, building and updating my blog, maintaining my social networking sites and much more. I love it!"

Many VAs have concentrated specialties (ah, a target niche!). Some specialize in bookkeeping, Internet marketing, social networking, or making cold calls; others focus on specific industries like real estate, travel, and legal.

Resources

There are many ways to locate a good Virtual Assistant. Ask people you know for a referral or check out the directories at *www.ivaa.org* or *www.assistu.com.*

12 Consider Outsourcing

You know that your business is moving ahead when you identify a need to outsource certain functions. When you don't have the capacity in-house to handle the load, outsourcing can be a cost-effective solution.

One way to cut costs is to hire contractors. These are independent workers who are business owners in their own right and are responsible for paying their own income taxes. Any contractor who works for you needs to receive a 1099 from you each year that shows how much you paid them.

The government has strict guidelines around the definition of a contractor versus an employee. For example, you cannot require a contractor to work a set schedule of hours like an employee would. If someone is reporting in to work between 8 to 5 each day, then according to the feds, that's an employee.

The use of contractors also depends on the nature of your business. In the construction industry, contracted workers are quite common. I hire writers and graphic designers on a contract basis for client projects. This has many benefits; I can control costs as the workload fluctuates, leverage a talented pool of writers and artists with different specialties, and avoid the costs and headaches of hiring employees.

A big consideration when deciding to outsource is how much your time is worth. If you earn $100 per hour and can hire someone to do the same task for $10, $25, or even $50 per hour, it makes sense to hire it out and free up your own time. Or, if you have a need for a service but not quite enough need to justify the cost of an employee, then outsourcing can often be a good option.

Following are some services that are commonly outsourced.

Marketing

Unless you have a background in marketing or some education on the field, this is a function that deserves professional assistance. From designing marketing collateral (flyers, brochures, postcards, and so forth) to the copy on your Website, marketing is an essential function for every business. Consider hiring a consultant, copywriter, graphic designer, Web designer, and/or a marketing firm to make sure your collateral is as professional as possible.

Accounting

I firmly believe that no business owner should be responsible for his own accounting. An expert bookkeeper or CPA will provide you with the added protection of having someone with you if and when you are ever audited. In addition, your accounting professional will likely save you money in the long run because she will be up to speed on all of the latest deductions and accounting laws, and will help you take advantage of those. This is an affordable service that deserves to be outsourced (unless you can afford to hire someone in-house to do it for you).

Information Technology (IT) Services

It can be costly to have staff dedicated to managing computers, and often it makes sense to hire an outside company for a fraction of the cost. If your business relies on computers to get work done—and most companies do today—having a comprehensive plan for backing up data, making sure computers are up and running, and having someone available in the event of a problem is essential to your bottom line. Check listings at your local chamber of commerce to find IT companies in your area.

Janitorial

Don't clean your own toilets. Period. You're reading this book because you want to take your business to the next level. Do you think that Bill Gates cleans the company bathroom? Hire it out!

13 Hire Employees

Hiring employees into a business for the first time is a big deal. Not only do you have the added complications and expense of payroll and worker's compensation insurance, but you have the added liability and potential headaches that go along with being the boss. However, don't let this deter you, because a need for employees means that your business is growing.

Crossing the Chasm to Employees

If your business is experiencing growth, there is a good chance that you are going to need to hire employees at some point. You will need to contact your business insurance provider to make sure your policies cover the employees and add worker's compensation insurance. It would be wise to inquire about the cost of this before you make someone an offer, because the costs of insurance can be debilitating in some industries.

In addition, you are going to need to process payroll. You would be wise to outsource this function to your accountant, or through your bank or a service provider such as Paychex (*www.Paychex.com*). Payroll means that you will have to withhold taxes and make deposits monthly and quarterly to state and federal accounts. (Nobody said this part would be fun.)

Before you begin your search to fill any position in your company, know what you are looking for. Identify skills, attitudes, and competencies that are important to the job function at hand. I also recommend having more than one person interview every candidate. If you run a one-person shop, ask a trusted peer to do you the favor of interviewing your candidate. We all see different things when we look into a kaleidoscope, so get as many perspectives as you can.

Before you make any hiring decisions, learn about the current labor laws where you live. You might also consider hiring an independent human resources consultant (as a contractor!) or an attorney to advise and assist you in making decisions. Labor laws are something that the government takes very seriously, so it is in your best interest that you do the same.

Resource

The U.S. Department of Labor has guidelines you must know before becoming an employer at *www.dol.gov/*.

 ## Manage Your Team

Ask business owners with a staff what their biggest challenges are and most will cite employee management. I know one business owner who sold his company primarily because he grew so tired of managing employee issues. There are a few lucky business owners who are naturals at this, but many find it challenging.

Here are some tips for better employee/management relations:

Set Expectations

Start by sharing your vision for your company and how each member fits in with that vision. If excellent customer service is important to your success, this should be engrained in the minds of your employees. Be very clear about what you expect in terms of performance, attitude, and anything that can impact your business. An employee manual is essential. Details on how to create one are coming up in this chapter.

Provide Incentive

Google is consistently rated one of the top companies to work for because of the amazing amenities provided to employees, including on-site daycare, dry cleaning, a fully-staffed cafeteria with free food, workout facilities, and much more.

Because you're a small business owner and probably can't afford extravagant incentives, look for other options. You could reward exceptional performance with an afternoon off or a gift certificate for a local restaurant. You might also consider offering profit-sharing bonuses based on company revenues and employee contributions. Holding a quarterly party for your staff with free food and activities can go a long way in cultivating employee satisfaction and loyalty.

Avoid Getting Too Friendly

Just as experts advise that we shouldn't take the role of friend with our kids, we should set similar boundaries with staff. You can and should like the people who work for you, but inviting them over for Sunday brunch each week is probably not a good idea.

Once friendship is established, the lines of authority are blurred. Employees may start to expect special treatment, and it will certainly be more difficult to deal with performance issues. If your style is to be the nice boss that everyone likes, make sure they also know that you are still the one in charge.

Just Say No to Family and Friends

It is nearly impossible to maintain a true boss/employee relationship with someone from your inner circle of life. Yet time and time again, business owners fall victim to the trap of hiring loved ones and then later regret the decision. Save yourself the heartache and avoid it if possible. If you do move in this direction, set clear expectations and boundaries early on.

Give Praise

By nature, humans want to receive praise. This desire is elevated in the workplace. Employees need to feel valued and appreciated. When someone does something well, say so. Studies have shown that employees often value recognition over dollars—yes, really! If you can get in the habit of appreciating employees, you can create goodwill that results in better performance all around.

Document Issues

Every employee should have a file that contains documentation for just about everything. Keep records of signed offer letters, performance reviews, and notes from doctors, and perhaps most importantly, document any issues that you have with the employee. If you have to discipline an employee, you have repeated performance discussions, or there is an issue with absenteeism, you will want to back it up with documentation in the event that you need to let the employee go.

Eventually we all have to let someone go, and there's nothing fun about that. But in today's lawsuit-happy world, you will want to have some proof of issues in case you end up in court. Of course you should be following those all-mighty labor board requirements, too.

Put Someone in the Middle

Several years ago when I was deep in the heart of loathing my employee management issues, I met Shari Fitzpatrick, owner of Shari's Berries. I asked her how she handled employee management issues and she replied, "Oh, I don't do any of that. I have a director who is in charge of managing employees."

If you decide that employee management isn't for you, build that vision into your organization chart. Hire a great person who can manage it for you.

Resources
- *1001 Ways to Reward Employees* by Bob Nelson
- *Love 'Em or Lose 'Em: Getting Good People to Stay* by Beverly Kaye
- *First, Break All the Rules: What the World's Greatest Managers Do Differently* by Marcus Buckingham

15 Assemble an Employee Manual

Large corporations use employee manuals to educate employees about policies and protect the company legally. Even if you have just one or two employees, a manual is a great tool for setting expectations and keeping your policies consistent.

An employee manual should always be reviewed by a lawyer to make sure it is compliant with local and federal laws. The following is a sample outline that you can use as a guideline for getting started:

1. Welcome and Introduction.
2. Purpose of Handbook.
3. Company Mission Statement.
4. Company History.
5. Employee Responsibilities and Code of Conduct.
6. Discipline Procedures.
7. Attendance and Punctuality.
8. Time Cards.
9. Work Hours, Breaks, and Lunch Breaks.
10. Overtime Policy.
11. Payday.
12. Payroll Deductions.
13. Performance Reviews and Wage Increases.
14. Promotions.
15. Resignation and Termination.
16. Telephone Usage.

17. Benefits Overview.
    a. Medical.
    b. Dental.
    c. Vision.
    d. Employee Assistance Program.
    e. Vacation.
    f. Sick Time.
    g. Tuition Reimbursement.
    h. Life Insurance.
    i. Disability Benefits.
    j. Employee Discount.
    k. Employee Referral Bonus.
    l. Years of Service Awards.
18. Leave of Absence.
19. Emergency Procedures.
20. Summary and Acknowledgement.
    a. Sick.
    b. Family Leave.
    c. Funeral.
    d. Disability.
    e. Jury Duty.
    f. Military.
    g. Maternity.
    h. Unpaid Leave.

Resource

Create Your Own Employee Handbook: A Legal and Practical Guide by Lisa Guerin, J.D.

16 Assemble an Operations Manual

An operations manual can act as a tool for training employees while empowering them to run your business effectively. Though it may seem like a lot of work, the effort put into your operations manual can save you money that could otherwise be wasted on mishandled procedures and employee training time.

When I owned my retail store, the operations manual was my ticket to freedom. It was filled with every possible scenario I could imagine and what to do about it. For example, there was a section on how to handle the business in the event of a power outage. There were also occasional procedures such as how to void a credit card transaction. That manual saved me countless phone calls from staff, as I spent very little time at the store and they often worked alone. When someone called looking for help, the first question I asked was, "Did you check the manual?"

Every operations manual is different, so yours should be tailored to your specific business needs. You may want to create separate manuals for each department or job description in your company. Your operations manual should grow and change with your business so make sure to update the contents often. Store the manual in a sturdy binder with dividers to keep it organized, making it easy to update the contents and replace pages when processes change. Also, consider asking your existing employees to assist in creating the manual by writing up their job descriptions and responsibilities.

The following is a suggested list of topics to address in your manual:

- Company Overview and History.
- Mission Statement.
- Opening Procedures.
- Closing Procedures.
- Cash Handling.
- Daily Tasks.
- Alarm System Operations.
- Safe Opening and Closing Procedures.
- Contact Numbers for Emergencies or Information.
- Employee Shift Coverage.
- Website Procedures.
- Customer Service Procedures.
- Sales Procedures.
- Sales Quotas.
- Commission Payments.
- Order Processing.
- Credit Card Processing.
- Refunds and Returns.

- Gift Certificates.
- Special Orders.
- Shipping and Receiving.
- Equipment Handling.
- Equipment Maintenance (replacing printer cartridges, receipt tape, etc.).
- Security Procedures.
- Emergency Procedures.
- Product Pricing and Discounts.
- Other Miscellaneous Procedures and Anything Specific to the Way Your Business Operates.

Don't forget to use your operations manual as a training tool for new hires. To make sure the information is accurate and valuable, ask your employees for feedback on the contents. Ask if they have questions about the topics covered and if the instructions are clear and easy to understand. Remember that this is a valuable business tool for you and your staff, so keeping it current should be a priority.

Success Interview
Shari Fitzpatrick

BerryFactory.com and Shari's Berries, Inc.

www.BerryFactory.com

Year Founded:	Shari's Berries: 1989, *BerryFactory.com*: 2006
Number of Employees:	Approximately 15 regular, up to 150 for holidays

What does your company do?

Creates, produces, and delivers the leading brand of chocolate-dipped strawberries (and related gifts) in the country.

Editor's note: Shari Fitzpatrick sold her original company, Shari's Berries, and subsequently launched BerryFactory.com. In addition to her Web presence, Shari also maintains several retail storefronts in the Sacramento area.

Shari's love affair with strawberries began as a little girl, with a strawberry patch her Father planted for her each summer. Strawberries quickly became her favorite fruit. Later, while working as a mortgage broker in Los Angeles, she began making potential clients handmade chocolate-dipped strawberries. The incredible popularity of these memorable edible gifts soon outpaced the success of her original career.

For almost 20 years, Shari's story and her creations have attracted international attention through appearances in O Magazine, In Style *magazine,* People *magazine, and* Chicken Soup for the Entrepreneur's Soul, *and on the* Today Show, The Apprentice, The Price Is Right, Wheel of Fortune, *and* QVC.

Describe a typical day in your life.

I work from my home office most days. I think my goal has always been to work from home so I can be here for my three boys—to get them off to school and be here for them when they return. My family is the most important thing to me, and my biggest fear is to wake up and have my boys grown and gone and have missed out on their upbringing. Life is short, and I'm so grateful I've realized that now.

My production center is more than an hour away from my home but, with today's technology, I can be one of those entrepreneurs who will conduct a conference call in my slippers and hair in a ponytail! My main jobs for my company are product development, marketing, and PR.

I usually schedule at least one day a week at my Sacramento office, to meet with my managers, view samples, and go over system details and anything new that's going on. During holidays like Valentine's Day (our busiest time of the year), I'll stay/live at a nearby hotel for an entire week.

Was there a specific turning point when you realized your business was moving to the next level?

For the first nine years, no. It was one day at a time, building a customer base year after year. Lots of hard work—and throwing spaghetti against the wall. After my ninth year I saw a great opportunity with the rise of Internet shopping. I brought in a partner and investors. At that point I saw us really taking off.

What processes or procedures have you implemented that have helped grow your company?

Technology. New enterprise system, Internet site, phone system, adding a call center to take overflow calls during the holidays, and streamlined production line systems. We produce 25 percent of our annual revenue during 2.5 days during Valentine's week. We had to expand to a large structure to capture all that we can and then quickly contract down to our normal size in order to not waste profits.

What are some of the best marketing strategies you have used to grow your company?

I am a firm believer in the importance of word-of-mouth, and offering a great product and great customer service to back it up. "The customer is ALWAYS right" is my motto. You never argue with a customer. We back our product with a 100-percent guarantee.

I enjoy trading my product for mentions/advertising. It's a win-win situation. For example, a radio station may trade advertising for berry credits with my company. Then they use the berry credit to send my product out to their top clients, who in turn get to experience my product and potentially become customers.

Are there any ways that you have leveraged the Internet to grow your business?

Totally.... We've practically become an Internet company as we ship our gourmet gifts nationwide, overnight, year-round! An ever-growing percentage of my business is converting to online ordering.

What challenges have you faced and how have you overcome them?

The objective of shipping a perishable and fragile product nationwide. To solve the challenge, I asked a lot of questions, performed a lot of tests and experiments, threw more spaghetti against the wall, and took chances.

How do you balance your work and personal life?

By always putting my family first and by having my priorities in order: God, family, and *then* work. My worst nightmare would be to wake up someday and have missed out on raising my boys. I can always work, but I have only one chance to be the best mom that I can be. Life truly does go by "like a blink of an eye." I'm so grateful that I realized that at a young age so I could truly take advantage of it.

I write everything down—all my thought, ideas, and so forth. This way it keeps my mind clear. It helps me to not forget things and to get projects done.

If you were starting over today, what would you do differently?

I would have never brought in partners; I would have done it alone. I needed to trust and believe in myself more early on.

CHAPTER 3

"In the business world the rearview mirror is always clearer than the windshield."

—Warren Buffett

Automate

17 Simplify With Checklists

The goal of any business on a growth path should be to simplify processes, and one of the quickest ways to do this is to utilize checklists. A checklist is a tool for ensuring consistency in every process in your business. It also helps employees deliver consistent service by making sure that every detail is managed.

Hotels are notorious for using checklists for cleaning rooms. Think about the number of details that must be tended to:

- Change sheets.
- Replace towels.
- Empty trash.
- Replace soap and bath products.
- Wipe down all surfaces.
- Place remote control on top of TV.
- Vacuum.
- Turn off lights.
- Set thermostat to 70 degrees.
- Place hotel manual next to phone.
- Check drawers and closets to ensure they are empty.
- Replace coffee supplies.
- Restock in-room bar.
- Place mint on pillow.

If any of these details are missed, the hotel guest will notice—and complain. Therefore, the cleaning attendants are provided with a list to ensure everything is handled properly.

Because I speak at a lot of events, I use a suitcase filled with materials so I can easily set up a display table. I learned early on that I needed a checklist to ensure I remembered to bring everything. It never fails; just when I think I don't need my list because I've remembered everything, I realize (when it's too late) that I forgot something.

There are a million ways to use checklists in your business. Here are a few ideas to get you started:

Prospect Form: When a prospect contacts your business, a checklist of questions to ask can help you qualify them and identify their needs.

Client Intake Form: If there is specific information you need from a new client, you can provide them with a form to fill out or use the form as an interview questionnaire to get the answers you need. This is similar to the paperwork you fill out at a doctor's office.

Project List: If a client project requires numerous steps, create a list of the actions needed, and identify who is responsible for each action and the target completion date.

Process List: If there are any processes in your business that require multiple steps for completion, put them on a list!

18 Answer the Phone—Seriously

Recently I received a message from a potential client who introduced herself as a life coach, which is an industry I have tremendous respect for. When I returned her call, I was greeted by a home answering machine, complete with a list of everyone in the household.

Right or wrong, I quickly decided that this person was not serious about her business. If she can't take her business seriously, how can she expect me or anyone else to do so?

Answering the phone is about as basic as it gets in business. In fact, I have often said that you can start a business with a computer, a phone, and a business card. It can be that simple. But how your phone is managed is another issue entirely.

I know owners of million-dollar companies who run their businesses from a cell phone. I see no problem with this, provided the voice-mail greeting is professional. I have an unlimited cell phone plan and often have my calls forwarded. It is a convenient, necessary, and valuable tool.

Nobody's Home

In a service business that relies on clients scheduling appointments, such as a health service provider or day spa, it is imperative that someone is answering the phone during business hours. I know of several businesses where the phone isn't always answered. It is wrongly assumed that the caller will leave a message and wait for a return call.

We are in living in a time of instant gratification, where our lives are moving faster than they ever have before. I don't know about you, but I don't have that kind of patience. If I just discovered an opening in my schedule and want to book a massage or a pedicure, I'm going to keep dialing until a human answers who can accommodate my request. If I have a chiropractic emergency, I don't have time to play phone tag. This is the kind of business that should undoubtedly invest in an answering service. The right service will pay for itself over and over again in increased bookings.

Other Solutions

If your business reaches a national audience, a toll-free number could be a wise investment. Services with your local phone company can cost as little as $5 per month and can be routed to your current business line.

Another interesting and low-cost alternative is an Internet phone service such as *Grasshopper.com.* Packages start at around $20 per month and include a toll-free number, a set number of airtime minutes, and the ability to create a professional phone tree. So if you have a few employees or if you want to designate different extensions for various service departments within your company, you can create extensions for each that are forwarded to your local office phone or even to cell phones. Each person in the tree has the ability to modify his/her settings, accept a call, or send a call to voice mail. Callers hear hold music during transfers, creating a professional image with a scalable and manageable solution. For a small fee, you can even hire professional voice talent to record your phone tree greeting.

The urgency, professionalism, and complexities of phone services vary for different types of businesses. Research your options carefully before making a decision. If you have to change your phone number down the road, that can present some challenges. Between notifying customers, updating your Website, and ordering new marketing materials and business cards, your phone number matters. How it is answered may be vitally important to your business. Choose wisely.

19 Leverage Your Bank

Having a relationship with your banker isn't just for the big guys. You may not see the value of this when your company is small, but, as you grow, having a relationship with a business specialist at your bank will come in handy.

I love that I can pick up the phone and call my banker with a quick question or request. I have opened accounts over the phone, sent e-mail requesting a temporary hold on a large deposit be lifted, and had small errors quickly repaired—all without ever leaving my desk. And when I need to apply for trade credit with a vendor, I know I have an ally at my bank who knows me and will be a great reference.

Your relationship with your banker can even turn into business opportunities. When your banker understands what you do, he or she can easily refer you to other clients. You may also be able to reserve the conference room at the bank for meetings or set up a temporary display in the lobby that showcases your business.

If you don't yet know the small business specialist at your bank, make a point of asking for an introduction the next time you are in the area. If there is no specialist available or you don't feel like this person wants to connect with you, then it may be time to seek out another bank. If you need a loan in five years, do you have confidence that your bank can help you with that?

Specialty Banks

Smaller community banks can often provide big benefits for small business customers. Some specialize in serving the business community, offering unique programs such as remote deposit acceptance (you can scan in checks from your office and never set foot in the bank), cash pick-up services, and specialized loan programs. They often have a staff devoted to making you feel like a valued client. What a concept!

It can be easy to get lost in the shuffle at a bigger commercial bank, so if you feel it's time for a change, investigate your options.

20 Use Online Bill Pay

I have to admit that I was a late adopter of the glorious freedom of paying my bills online. I used to spend hours each month paying bills. It was an ordeal I dreaded and often put off because I hated it so much. Paying bills online is about as easy as it gets.

Your bank should offer this service for free. You can set up your payees to include account numbers and mailing addresses. You can designate bills to auto-pay so you never have to worry about them, or you can quickly log in, key in a payment amount, and hit "Send." Voila!

When I acquire a new vendor, I quickly add it to the system when making the first payment. The bank mails out a computer-generated check and I'm done. Future payments take just seconds to issue.

To make life even easier and because I hate dealing with accounting, I have granted my accountant access to log in to my account to reconcile my statements. If she has a question about an entry, she can view the details of each payment issued, saving us both a call. Everything should be this easy!

21 Evaluate Business Software

Software is something we use to make life easier. Most of us have grown accustomed to using basic office tools like Microsoft Word and Excel, but there may be other solutions that could improve the efficiency of your business.

Suzi Sherman, co-owner of Arch Technologies, an IT company in Sacramento, learned this lesson the hard way: "We spent some time developing an internal ticket tracking system to manage our workload. The problem with programming for entrepreneurs is that our vision grows. We're always coming up with new ideas. But we were spending so much time working on the inside, that we weren't focused on selling outside."

"We decided to go out and buy a solution instead of create it ourselves. It included CRM [customer relationship management], project management, ticket tracking, dispatch, and a customer portal so that customers can create their own tickets," says Sherman. "We have to treat our business like a client sometimes and really try to find an answer and be objective about it.

It just didn't make sense to build it ourselves and we learned a lot from that experience, which benefits us and our customers."

A lot of problems can be solved with the right software. From workflow automation and customer relationship management to helpdesk software and sales force automation, there are abundant choices available to you.

Resource

If you want to test drive software programs, you can't beat the free downloads available through C-NET. Here you can find pre-screened trials of everything from contact management programs and helpdesk applications to spreadsheet templates and video games. Check out *download.cnet.com.*

22 Manage Computer Issues (Before They Manage You)

Is there anything more frustrating than dealing with technology issues? It's a colossal time-waster, to say the least, when something goes wrong and you don't know how to fix it. And for most of us, our computers are essential to business operations. So why do so many businesses take chances with their technology?

Disaster Recovery 101

If you do nothing else, please, please, please back up your data. What will happen to your business when your hard drive crashes? What if you can't recover your files? How will your clients be affected? How will it impact your bottom line? Too many people learn this lesson the hard way.

Aside from a technical meltdown, your computer could be stolen or damaged in a disaster (earthquake, flood, fire). You can purchase a backup drive and easily automate the copying of your files each day. I also recommend taking it a step further by backing up your data off-site. This is what the big companies do.

They back up their data to huge data centers in cities far away so that, if disaster strikes, the company won't be out of commission.

Companies like *Connected.com* automate your backups to occur each day. You can also create a disaster recovery boot disk, which would essentially allow you to easily restore your system in the event of a catastrophic failure. Please do not ignore this warning. Just imagine the consequences.

IT Services for Small Businesses

Whether you are a company of one or many, if computers make it all happen for you, you need to know who to call *before* you need to make the call. For a small office, this may be a matter of locating a local repair shop and learning about its capabilities and services. Ask how quickly the shop can repair a problem. I once had my main computer crash on a Saturday, and my local shop had me up and running before the sun went down. You might also consider hiring an independent computer whiz who makes house calls.

If you have more than a handful of computers, it's time to investigate hiring an IT company. A wide variety of service levels are available to manage simple problems like software installation and parts replacement to complex issues like building a wireless network.

If you ever relocate your office and have several computers to transfer, a good IT company can build a plan to make your move quick and painless. The company will ensure that your data lines are wired properly and that you experience minimal downtime. This service will be essential to your business.

23 Upgrade E-mail

If you're still logging on to AOL or Hotmail to check e-mail, it's time for an upgrade. These programs are fine for personal use, but they lack professionalism in the business world. Your entire staff should have e-mail addresses based on the company domain. This is a very minor expense and projects a more professional image to your clients and partners.

In addition, the free e-mail tools don't offer integration with programs like Microsoft Outlook. Ideally your e-mail provider should offer POP access so that you can use a professional management tool to handle folders, sort and find information, and keep track of your contacts.

 ## Success Interview
Patricia Beckman
Cybertary, Inc.
Roseville, California
www.Cybertary.com and
www.CybertaryFranchise.com

Year Founded:	2005
Business Partners:	1
Number of Employees:	4

What does your company do?

A Cybertary is a highly skilled professional working as a Virtual Assistant (VA) to provide administrative support and specialized services to businesses, entrepreneurs, executives, and busy people.

What led you to start your business?

I spent 20 years in the corporate workforce in various financial management rolls. In my final corporate position, I managed a team of financial analysts across the western United States, and traveled three days per week managing my team and teaching project managers how to read financial reports. Honestly, I had a nice paycheck and a great collection of suits, but my children did not even know what I did for a living. Nor did they care; they just knew that I was gone a lot.

My "a-ha" moment was when I was making lunch for my daughters one day and realized that I did not know which girl preferred ketchup and which wanted tartar sauce. I realized I had lost touch with my girls in many ways: I did not know their friends, I missed dance recitals and parent/teacher conferences, and they no longer came to my side of the bed in the middle of the night because I wasn't usually there. I realized that the price I was paying to have the nice paycheck was way too high. I quit my job the week of the "fish sticks incident" and sought a way to get home to be available for my family.

Was there a specific turning point when you realized your business was moving to the next level?

My original business plan was based on a client base of five to seven active, recurring clients that I would manage myself. I launched November 1, 2005, and gained five clients my first week. I then started to gain five to seven new client leads per week and found that I needed to add at least one team member per month to keep up with the client demand.

I discovered that due to the branding, Website, and marketing materials I had created, people *presumed* Cybertary was a franchise and started to ask me where I heard about Cybertary and how they could get into a Cybertary business, and assumed that we were an enormous nationwide company. We began getting huge volumes of resumes every week from moms who wanted to join the team, and from clients who wanted our services...but I was at maximum capacity and could not manage the workload for that many clients and team members independently.

After a while I took the hint, and decided to turn the Cybertary business model into a franchise opportunity. This way we could continue to meet the growing client demand and we could provide more opportunities for moms, disabled, and caregivers to work from home at a professional wage. Franchisees can also outsource work to other franchisees based on client needs and skill levels of team members, so that we are each individually doing what we do best. Now people can own their Cybertary business, add their own teams, and service their own client base using the Cybertary branding and infrastructure.

We launched the franchise opportunity in April 2007, and now have four active franchisees in two states, plus a Regional Developer. Cybertary has grown into a network of professional Virtual Assistants, primarily served by stay-at-home moms. Cybertary assists small businesses and entrepreneurs who have realized they can't "do it all" and have balance. Cybertary also gives enterprising stay-at-home moms, or dads, the opportunity to utilize their professional skills and find work/life balance.

What processes or procedures have you implemented that have helped grow your company?

Our intranet system serves as a centralized communication and collaboration vehicle for all franchisees. It is one of the primary tools that our franchisees use on a daily basis to access to up-to-date information about their business 24/7.

The Home page works like a "dashboard" to instantly see Team Calendar & Workload, Document and File Storage Library, Contact Management, work collaboration tools, Discussion forums, e-mail messaging, our powerful skill search database, and more.

We have also documented every procedure and continue to evolve our documentation as issues arise. This allows for consistency of operations franchise-wide, which translates to a consistent customer experience.

What are some of the best marketing strategies you have used to grow your company?

From day one of Cybertary's existence when it was just me and my handful of clients, all of our marketing materials have had a professional quality that made us look like a big company. This gave us a few advantages:

❧ Because you never get a second chance to make a first impression, and because our marketing materials are our first impression, having quality materials and Website gave us a professional advantage over the competition.

❧ When we did grow, we did not have to reinvent all of our marketing materials to accommodate our expansion.

Are there any ways that you have leveraged the Internet to grow your business?

As an Internet-based company, both the franchisees and the Cybertary Corporate office use the Internet to the best of our ability to increase brand recognition and drive customer interest and traffic to our Websites. Some of our strategies include:

❧ Our proprietary Cybertary intranet gives all of our franchisees and team members instant online access to Team Calendar & Workload, Document and file storage library, Contact Management, work collaboration tools, Discussion forums, e-mail messaging, and our powerful skill search database. The intranet becomes a centralized communication and collaboration vehicle for all franchisees. It serves as one of the primary tools that our franchisees use on a daily basis to access to up-to-date information about their business 24/7.

❧ We have a professional Website that is continuously evolving with fresh content.

❧ Search engine optimization of *Cybertary.com* and *CybertaryFranchise.com.*

- Pay-per-click marketing for both *CybertaryFranchise.com* and for each individual franchisee. The franchisees post PPC ads that are focused on the local area of their franchise.

- Franchisees gain access to an unlimited, online continuing education portal so that they can learn new skills to expand their services offering, or keep their skills current as technology evolves.

- We distribute monthly e-mail newsletters as opposed to the more costly print form newsletters.

- Our franchisees utilize online social networking: LinkedIn, Plaxo, Facebook, and so on.

- Blogging.

- Drip e-mail campaigns to potential franchisees.

- Online forum presence—within the small business online world and the virtual assisting community.

What challenges have you faced and how have you overcome them?

As the founding Cybertary, the first nine months that I assembled the business foundation before looking for my first client were very difficult and required a significant investment in time and money. Many people overlook the importance of laying the initial business foundation before they launch their business, and may struggle to catch up and never have an opportunity to regain momentum.

I overcame this challenge on behalf of our Cybertary franchisees by documenting everything and developing the Cybertary business model into a "turnkey" operation so that our franchisees don't have to endure the same startup curve. All of their marketing materials, legal agreements, forms, infrastructure, and accounting systems are ready to go so that a franchisee can be open for business with a fully functional operation in as little as six weeks.

If you were starting over today, what would you do differently?

I wouldn't do anything different, really. I have learned quite a bit from my mistakes, and I wear them proudly. Each mistake we make is another opportunity to improve. I study our errors, document them for our franchisee's edification, and create systems to avoid them in the future.

Some of my learning opportunities have included:

❧ Making unwise marketing investments, such as costly trade show exhibition at events that don't draw our target audience, or print ads in publications that were not appropriate. I now thoroughly study each marketing alternative diligently to determine audience and cost per lead from each alternative.

❧ Not seeking help sooner. When I was in the process of turning Cybertary into a franchise, I was simultaneously running the business of supporting clients and managing a team. During that time I was essentially working two full-time jobs, and as a result I was not performing as well as I should at either of them. Eventually I recognized that I needed to let some things be managed by others so I could keep focused, perform well, and maintain my own work/life balance.

❧ Computer data backups! We have always been diligent about performing backups to both an external hard drive and a remote online service, but we have seen several of Cybertary clients businesses endure major setbacks or even failure because of a computer crash and data loss.

What advice do you have for other business owners?

Any business should be run like a business...not like a hobby. Even if you are a solopreneur, have regular monthly meetings with yourself to review your financial statements, set measureable and achievable goals for the coming weeks and months, and strategize your business growth.

CHAPTER 4

"Your most unhappy customers are your greatest source of learning."

—Bill Gates

Your Client Goldmine

24 Identify Low-Hanging Fruit

Low-hanging fruit represents your easiest opportunities to generate business. What a lot of business owners forget is that current and past customers are low-hanging fruit. If they have done business with you before, they are quite likely to do business with you again.

You must remind your customers that your business exists and introduce them to new offers. You can do this with newsletters, direct mail campaigns, phone calls, note cards, invitations to events—the point is to touch them on a regular basis.

The owners of my local auto shop do this very well. They send quarterly postcards that remind me it's time for an oil change. In addition, they send a periodic newsletter and call after each service to inquire about my satisfaction with their service. I no longer even think about whether or not it's time to service my car, because I count on them to remind me.

When it comes to retailers, e-mail marketing can be a great strategy for staying top of mind. I love to shop online. With my busy lifestyle, it's convenient for me to peruse the online racks in the middle of the night. I will happily subscribe to e-mail announcements from my favorite retailers so that I know what's new and what's on sale.

On the flip side, I am amazed by service providers who do a job and then disappear. A few years ago, I had my air conditioner serviced at home. The technician was friendly and I was pleased with his work. The following year, I wanted to have another preventative check done before Sacramento hit triple digits on the thermometer. I couldn't remember the name of the company I had used the previous year because I never heard from it again. The company could have sent me a postcard reminding me that it was time for service or it could have sent a couple of mailings so that the brand stuck in my over-crowded mind. Instead, the company lost the sale because I had to start from square one.

How can you be at "top of mind" with your customers? Better yet, how can you provide value at the same time?

25 Solicit Feedback

Because customers are the life-blood of every business, knowing what they want and need can mean the difference between a new product that soars to success and one that flops as quickly as it is introduced. In the 1980s, Coca Cola reformulated its flagship soda and launched a huge marketing campaign for "New Coke." The public response to the new brand bordered on outrage. It turned out that customers didn't want the classic version of Coke to change, a lesson the company learned the hard way. Coca Cola could have saved a lot of time, trouble, and money by asking a large cross-section of customers for feedback before changing the product.

As entrepreneurs, many of us are natural idea-generators. I have experienced many sleepless nights mulling over an idea that I thought was great, only to realize later on that my hot idea wasn't so hot.

A great way to solicit feedback from customers is to conduct a survey. These can be done in person, by phone, by mail, or via e-mail. One tool that I use for conducting surveys online is *www.SurveyMonkey.com.* The service is free for up to 10 questions and 100 responses, and more extensive surveys can be conducted for a reasonable fee. You can send the survey link out via e-mail, list it on your Website or blog, and even promote it through your social networking channels like Facebook or Twitter.

Surveys have many advantages. Customers like to know that their voices are being heard. The results can be instrumental in guiding a small business to big opportunities. You can even publish survey results in a white paper or feature them in your newsletter so your customers know you're listening to them.

26 Build Relationships That Last

During my years in the Silicon Valley, I was recruited from a customer-service position into software sales. I worked with big-name dotcoms and was successful in selling large contracts and building key relationships, yet I had the least sales experience of any person on the sales force.

I am convinced that my commitment to customer service set me apart. I wanted to know my customers on a personal level. I would invite them to lunch and, instead of spending the hour talking about software and computer issues, I would learn about their spouses and children and what they did over the weekend. Relationships grew naturally and sales followed.

Years later, I still hear from many of my past clients—key executives from large companies. Social networking has made it easier than ever to stay connected, and we are able to keep in touch and maintain a genuine connection.

When you're a small business owner, every customer matters. Yet with so many responsibilities, it can be easy to lose sight of the importance of building relationships that go the distance.

Try This

➤ Make it a habit to connect with people authentically. Ask questions and show interest in who they are and what matters to them.

➤ Pick up the phone and say hello once in a while.

➤ Schedule non-meetings such as lunch, a coffee date, a golf outing, or a baseball game.

➤ Don't try too hard; people will notice. Treat the relationship just as you would any other relationship: with genuine interest.

27 Show Appreciation

Showing appreciation for your clients can set you apart from your competitors, increase loyalty, improve retention, inspire sales, and build relationships that last a lifetime. Reaching out to your clients is also an opportunity to remind them that your business exists. Effective marketing relies on repeat exposure and showing appreciation is an affordable and effective way to keep your marketing wheels in motion.

One note of caution: Some companies and industries have strict guidelines about accepting gifts. This is especially true of media professionals and government workers. Gifts can be construed as bribes, so, when in doubt, ask your clients if such policies exist or stick to sending items with no monetary value.

Following are client-appreciation strategies that can help you cultivate client retention.

1. **Greeting Cards:** *The Guinness Book of World Records* lists Joe Girard, a car salesman from Detroit, as the world's best salesman. Girard earned the honor by selling 18 cars in a single day. One of his secrets to success is sending 12 cards per year to every single customer and prospect. There are dozens of major and minor holidays throughout the year, and each provides a great reason to send a card.

2. **Personal Notes:** Thoughtful and unexpected thank-you notes can be sent after client appointments, following a purchase, or whenever a client has done anything deserving some

appreciation. Although sending an e-mail may be quick and easy, you will make a lasting impression by sending a handwritten note in the mail.

3. **Invitations:** Spending time together outside of the office gives you a chance to cultivate the relationship by getting to know each other better. Consider inviting your top contacts to lunch, dinner, sporting events, charity functions, or other events where you can spend time together.

4. **Small Gifts:** Flowers, books, a mug full of candy, and other token items can make thoughtful gifts for clients. These can be sent on special occasions such as birthdays, holidays, or anniversaries, or can be sent for no reason other than to show your gratitude.

5. **Food:** Everyone loves food. Consider sending cupcakes from your local bakery, providing a catered lunch at your client's office, or dropping off a tray of cookies.

6. **Gift Cards:** Sending gift cards for items or places your clients will enjoy can have an added benefit: they will think of you when it comes time to redeem the gift! Options include coffee shops, restaurants, movie theaters, book stores, office supplies stores, or anything else your clients would appreciate. For even more mileage, consider partnering with another business and send each other's gift cards.

7. **Customer-Appreciation Days:** Designate one or more days each year to celebrate your clients. You could offer a customer-only secret promotional sale, give away lunch if you have a physical location, or provide a special bonus to those on your mailing list.

8. **The Gift of Information:** E-books, reports, workbooks, videos and other types of information products can make great gifts. For example, compile a list of useful tips that your customers will appreciate and either deliver it via e-mail in a

PDF document or publish it in booklet format to mail or hand out.

9. **Life Events:** If you know that your client is getting married, having a baby, being promoted or enjoying another major life event, send an acknowledgment—even if it is a simple card. Your gesture will be noticed and appreciated.

10. **Host Events:** Host a party or an open house at your office or a restaurant. If your clients are geographically dispersed, you can hold a virtual event by inviting them to participate in complimentary online seminars.

28 Generate and Reward Referrals

We are all influenced by recommendations from others. When your friend raves about a book he is reading, there's a good chance you will feel compelled to read it, too. When someone buzzes about a great new restaurant, you will probably make a mental note to eat there.

If you are researching preschools for your child or seeking a new hairdresser, you are probably going to ask around for recommendations. If you're planning a vacation, you may ask friends for suggested things to do there or places to eat. We naturally want to help each other find the best options and use our time and money wisely.

With that in mind, what is going to hold more weight: an advertisement in the phone book or a recommendation from a friend? Here are some ways to spark referrals from your clients.

Start With a Question

Your existing clients are an ideal source of referrals to your business and, in many cases, all you need to do is ask: "Hey, Joe. I'm so glad you're happy with the new driveway we paved for you. Do you know anyone else who needs some work done? I would be grateful if you could help spread the word about our business."

Because Joe is a satisfied customer, simply asking the question could lead to several new opportunities. Joe may have several neighbors who also need your services. He could visit his sister the following week and notice her driveway is cracked. He will remember to recommend you simply because you asked.

Offer to Send a Mail Announcement

A couple of years ago when my mom moved in to a new house, her real estate agent offered two smart services. First, he printed up "I have a new address" cards that she could send to her friends and family. At the bottom of each card was his contact information. Second, he offered to host a housewarming party. He provided the invitations, food, and beverages, and helped her welcome her loved ones in her new home—all while he had the opportunity to personally meet and greet all of the attendees. Smart move!

Provide Incentive

One local roofing company recently mailed out a postcard campaign offering $100 for referrals. If you referred someone who then purchased a new roof, you would receive $100 in cash. Given the high cost of a new roof, paying $100 for a referral was an inconsequential expense for the roofing company in exchange for drumming up new business.

Hair salons and spas often benefit from providing incentives. My local salon mails me a $20 gift certificate for every new client I refer. I enjoy receiving the benefit and, given the long-term value of a new client to a salon, $20 is a worthwhile way to inspire customers to spread the word.

Reverse Referrals

If your clients are business owners, look for ways to refer business to them. This is an unexpected gesture that will not only make them grateful to you, but can inspire them to want to return the favor.

29 Implement a Loyalty Program

Loyalty programs are nothing new, though I believe they are under-utilized and a missed opportunity for many companies. Big retailers use them to bring customers back again and again. The ultimate goal should be to give customers a reason to remain loyal to your business and prevent them from going to the competition.

Here are some examples:

➤ **Safeway Club Card:** Safeway provides shoppers with an opportunity to get a free club card. In order to qualify, you must provide your contact information (helping the company build a massive database). When you swipe your card at checkout, you receive a discount on special promotional items and accumulate points. Those points can be used to save on gas at Safeway gas stations and occasionally the company offers special bonuses for card holders.

➤ **Ulta Rewards:** This beauty retailer tabulates dollars spent on shampoo, makeup, and other personal care products, and allows the card holder to apply points toward dollars off from future purchases. Because those points directly equate to dollars at the register, members of this program have added incentive to buy all of their personal care products in one place.

➤ **Starbucks Gold:** In 2008 Starbucks introduced a gold card program. For $20 per year, members get save 10 percent off of purchases for the year. If you spend more than $200 per year at Starbucks, this card is a deal. You can also register your card online to receive additional bonuses on your birthday and announcements about card holder specials.

There are plenty of businesses that use less-sophisticated loyalty programs. One of my favorite restaurants recently launched a lunch club. The lunch club card is printed on business card stock and gets stamped with each meal. After you have six lunches, you get the seventh free.

I love this idea for restaurants for several reasons. First, they can use club cards to fill the house during slow times. A restaurant that has a booming breakfast business could have a dinner club card and vice versa. Also, people rarely dine alone, so most club members are going to bring a friend. That friend can then enroll in the program. And so on, and so on, and so on.

How to Use a Loyalty Program in Your Business

If you want to follow the card-swipe model, start by talking to your merchant card service provider. Some offer the ability to track sales and create similar programs. A quick Google search also reveals a long list of companies that provide this kind of service.

Punch cards are also easy and inexpensive to create. Print them up on business card stock through a service like *VistaPrint.com* and then have a secure way to punch them. (A unique hole punch with a picture of a star, animal, or other image can be found at a local crafts store.)

Here are some other ideas for implementing loyalty programs:

➤ A florist could offer an upgraded bouquet after six deliveries in a calendar year.

➤ A carpet cleaner could provide one free room when services are used four times within a year.

➤ A dry cleaner could give $10 off after you spend $100 on services.

➤ A gas station could provide a free car wash for every five fill-ups.

➤ A children's boutique could give away a free book with purchases of more than $100.

➤ A staffing agency could provide employers with four free hours of labor for every 80 hours contracted.

➤ A fitness center could provide two free hours of personal training for every year of membership.

30 Turn Problems Into Opportunities

Nobody aims to have disgruntled customers, but it happens. What you may not realize is that an angry customer presents an opportunity. If you can turn a bad situation around—if you can rescue an unhappy client—you can actually build loyalty that you didn't have before.

Here's another lesson I picked up in the Silicon Valley. During the dotcom boom, it was my job to deal with high-visibility clients. I fielded calls in the middle of the night when something went wrong.

The company I worked for provided key software that was meant to keep computers running no matter what, but nothing is flawless. So when the software didn't do its job, I had to find a solution to the problem. I reeled in technical support—the big guns—the most skilled people who would find the solutions for our customers as quickly as possible. This rapid response in the eye of the storm turned out to be a powerful relationship-building tool.

We became the heroes. Often times a crisis involved multiple vendors, yet our goal was to be first on the scene, to be the most responsive, and to be proactive whenever possible. Through time our customers learned that they could count on us. Sometimes a problem was our fault; sometimes it wasn't. But no matter what, we showed up as advocates and did what was needed to get the job done. It put us in the position of trusted advisor. Soon customers were turning to us for advice on their other vendor choices. We were not infallible, but we demonstrated our commitment—and that can go a long way.

An unhappy customer does not have to turn into a lost customer. Here are some ways to turn a problem into an opportunity:

Empathize With the Client

Though it may be difficult to keep a tight lip, just listen and let your customer vent. Listening allows you to determine what the customer is really angry about. Is it the actual problem that is causing his rage, or is it how your customer looks to his superiors? Determine what the customer is really asking for and figure out how to deliver the solution. If higher-level management needs to be addressed, this creates an opportunity for you to set up a meeting and establish a relationship. If your customer's business is being impacted, then you need to take quick action to find a resolution.

Establish a Plan of Action

If a resolution to a problem is going to take some time, form a plan. Schedule meeting times or conference calls with your customer and explain the progress. Assure him/her that a resolution is in sight and then do whatever it takes to find that solution.

Move up the Food Chain

Set up a meeting with your contact and his superiors. Bring in your own management team and use this opportunity to show everyone involved how you are going to take action. Outline the plan for resolution and commit to updating everyone involved as your progress toward resolution. Then be sure to follow up and deliver on your promises.

A meeting like this lets you meet executives and work your way up the organization chart, laying the foundation for future opportunities. Though you are meeting under unfortunate circumstances, once the problem is resolved, you will be remembered for your quick action and excellent customer service.

Offer a Concession

When something goes wrong, it's a good idea to make a peace offering. You could also coordinate a dinner or trip to a ball game to thank your new executive contacts for their patience and time. Does your company have a user's group meeting, trade show, or annual conference coming up? Offer some free passes. Attendance at events like these almost always leads to a sale. Though you can simply hand over a gift certificate or gift, considers options that could lead to future business.

By exceeding their expectations, providing excellent customer service, and showing customers that you follow through on your commitments, you can build tremendous loyalty. It's the best way to build trust and a lasting relationship and, before you know it, your most disgruntled customer could become your best client.

 ## Success Interview

Sandra Yancey

eWomenNetwork

www.eWomenNetwork.com

Year Founded:	2000
Number of Employees:	25 employees and 115 contractors

What does your company do?

We consider ourselves the number-one resource for connecting and promoting women in business. We are a marketing and promotion machine for women business owners and women in organizations who are responsible for their firms.

We create a forum for women to meet other like-minded women who believe that success is about sharing resources, leads, and tools. The more we help each other be successful, the more we will be successful.

Was there a specific turning point when you realized your business was moving to the next level?

I started thinking about starting this business in 1998 and then began working on the business model and business plan. I did a series of focus groups, hired a firm to validate my concept, and hired a company to do the Website.

Originally it was supposed to be purely online networking—and remember, this was before social networking was around. I wanted to create a profile database so that women could interact and connect with each other through the World Wide Web. In the focus groups, the women said that this sounded great. When I asked about chapter meetings, they said they were too busy.

When eWomenNetwork was about five months old, I heard from a woman in Alpharetta, Georgia, just outside of Atlanta. She said she met another member who lived in Duluth and they were going to meet at a coffee house. She was checking to see if there were any other members in the area who might like to join them. That's when I started to shift my business model—because you have to sell the way your customers buy.

I was going broke, just short of bankruptcy. I was just way before my time. Online was such a hard sell because it was still relatively new. The growth wasn't moving fast enough compared to the cost of what it took to run it. Then I started seeing women picking up the phone and finding ways to connect.

I didn't know anything about how to run chapters. I felt like I had to differentiate myself from chambers and other groups; I felt like it had to have its own unique philosophy. I was the first managing director and held events at the country club here in Dallas. I got it trademarked and went through the process so that I could speak to how it was different. And I thought, "I can train other women to do this."

We're going through a growth spurt right now and adding five managing directors a month; we have almost 90 managing directors. We also have an annual conference, and I was a little worried about registration because of the economy. But at this moment we have well over 500 more women registered than we did last year at this time.

What I'm starting to believe is that there is a huge underestimation out there about how starved women are to be in an environment that really is positive and uplifting and hopeful and powerful and valuable. I just think that it's so negative out there. The conference is hopeful, inspirational, and positive. It's a winning formula.

What processes or procedures have you implemented that have helped grow your company?

You have to constantly revise and change and grow. It's all about process. I continue to refine the managing director program. We continue to build the technology—the back engine for how our members register. We recently launched individual chapter Websites.

We tell our managing directors that they can't do it all alone and, to really grow the chapter, they need a leadership team. And the conference has expanded. In the past it's been four days, but we are announcing for the first time a free pre-conference day.

We are also launching our own social network and blogging, and we're doing our meetings with managing directors in a webinar fashion. They aren't even picking up their phone; they listen and watch from their computers.

We have traditionally focused on national sponsorships. Now we're getting into regional and local sponsorships. Before we were too small to manage all of that. We're also watching the way our customers buy. They are redirecting budgets to regional and local levels and we're working on that.

We're aggressively opening chapters in more cities—200 cities by the end of this year. Ultimately our customers are our members. We need to do everything we can to over-deliver. Managing directors need to be introducing them to new people every month. We're developing training around those core competencies.

What are some of the best marketing strategies you have used to grow your company?

The greatest, most powerful strategy is what I call the "whisper" campaign. Women are spreading the word for us. We have also invested in some great search engine optimization techniques.

We are developing more and more affiliate relationships for cross-pollination of the message of eWomenNetwork. We also have great feet on the street through our managing directors. And we have a business matchmaker program so when a member refers three new members, she gets a free display table and time in front of the audience.

We also have the ABC radio show with a national audience. And I spend a decent chunk of time doing interviews for magazines and television programs. Just this week we got a call from *Good Morning America.*

Last year while I was in Puerto Rico on vacation, Donnie Deutch from *The Big Idea* called. I was due to leave the next day, and I told them that there was no way I could get there. But I had to make it happen. So I called my girlfriend, walked her through my closet and had her pick out my outfit and shoes. She shipped my clothes to New York and when I arrived the next day, I changed out of my casual vacation clothes and into interview clothes and went on the air. The media is in the business of inconvenience; it's rarely around your schedule. When it comes to marketing, you have to seize the opportunities.

If you were starting over today, what would you do differently?

I would go and get money before I needed it. Nobody told me that in the beginning. I would also build relationships a lot faster. I would swallow my own medicine.

I was embarrassed about how hard the business was at the beginning and how long it took me to get it ramped up. I just didn't want to tell people that I wasn't making any money. You have to surround yourself with an A-team—a great core set of people. You have to be open and honest about what's going on, take their advice, adapt it, and take action.

I would learn the difference between "busy-ness" and business. I was exhausted and I was very busy. The rejection was so great for me and I kept myself busy. I was getting poorer and poorer every day. In the beginning, you've got to do the really hard work. Once I shifted that, things changed.

I would also put myself on the payroll sooner. For me, it was validating and made me feel legit. I would hire staff sooner. I waited until I was almost comatose with exhaustion. Then once I got help, I realized that she could do all the things that were keeping me busy so I could focus on all the things that made the cash register ring. And once she was on the payroll, that alone made me get serious because I knew I had to make payroll. It was amazing what I could make happen on Thursday afternoon when payroll was due on Friday.

What advice do you have for other business owners?

I think success is all about three things: The first one is relationships, the second one is relationships, and the third one is relationships.

First, you have to take inventory of the people in your life that are valuable and you have to feed them and love them and take care of them. Invest time and energy to nurture those relationships.

The second key is about the relationships with people you have yet to meet. You need to constantly be meeting new people; they give you *access.* You can have the greatest business model, a business plan, and a beautiful Website with all the bells and whistles, yet none of that will make you successful. In the end, success is about relationships and getting access to the next contact, lead, opportunity. People are what give you access. You need to constantly be meeting new people.

Third, take an inventory of all of the toxic, draining, dysfunctional relationships that are weighing you down and holding you back from your dream. It's not necessary to try to convert them or have a falling out, but start by recognizing that it's not serving you well. Give them a hug and make space. When you create distance, the universe now knows that you have space in your life. That opens the lock that opens the door that leads you to your dream come true.

Part Two

Execute
(Take Action)

CHAPTER 5

"Lack of money is no obstacle. Lack of an idea is an obstacle."

—Ken Hakuta, Inventor

Money Management

31 Cash: Get It Before You Need It

While interviewing business owners for this book, over and over again many said they wished they had gotten access to money before they needed it. When cash flow gets tight, it can be much harder to find relief.

Here are some options:

➤ **Business Loan:** Start by inquiring about options with your bank. The Small Business Administration (*www.sba.gov*) can also provide assistance. Additional options include *www.ibank.com,* which allows you to submit an application to numerous banks, and *www.superiorfg.com.* Women-owned businesses can find options at *www.countmein.org.* Lending communities like *www.Prosper.com* and *www.Zopa.com* facilitate private loans.

➤ **Business Line of Credit:** This is similar to opening an equity line on your house. You only pay for it if you use it and should apply through your bank.

➤ **Business Grant:** Nonprofits are more likely to get substantial funding from grants, but smaller grants are available for some small businesses. Check out *www.grants.gov.*

➤ **Venture Capital and Angel Investors:** Venture capital is a major investment, often by a private firm or group of investors, who believe a business has a bright future and the right plans to take it there. Angel investors are similar to VCs, though they can be private individuals looking for investment opportunities. Resources for locating VC firms include *capital-connection.com, www.nvca.org/,* and *www.activecapital.org/.*

➤ **Factoring:** A factoring service will effectively pay you cash based on your outstanding receivables, and will take a big chunk in fees in return. Factoring is usually a last resort for cash flow when things are desperate. I did speak to one business owner who admitted to using factoring in her early years until she was able to land some much bigger clients and get back on track. Her business eventually grew into a multi-million-dollar enterprise, though I suspect her results are not typical.

➤ **Private Investor:** A private investor is a partner, whether silent or active, who invests in the business. This could be a relative, friend, peer, or even a competitor.

32 Manage Bookkeeping and Payroll

I am a writer. I like words, and I hate numbers. When I first ventured into entrepreneurial life, I took a QuickBooks class and quickly remembered how much I hated anything to do with accounting (flashback to college accounting class and the agony of trying to get through the final exam). I immediately hired an accountant.

Since my first week in business, I have been sending my receipts and statements off to my accountant each month. She tells me when to pay my taxes and how much to send. She keeps me apprised of new laws and requirements. When the IRS called, she saved my tail.

Enter Payroll

When I hired my first employees, I had no idea how complicated it was going to be. Aside from the added headache and expense of worker's compensation insurance and learning labor laws, I had to contend with payroll.

Payroll has its own unique set of headaches. From withholding taxes and depositing them on a schedule to state and federal reporting requirements and issuing W2s, payroll is a giant pain in the rear. Handing this over to my accountant was a welcome relief. I know that I am compliant, that checks are going out on time, and that I don't have to worry. That is worth its weight in gold.

Today there are many options for payroll management. Services are offered by banks, bookkeepers, accountants, or specialty companies such as Paychex. All I know is that I wouldn't have it any other way.

The moral of this story is an obvious one. Sure, you can keep your books yourself. You can also use software and manage your own payroll. If you somehow find this therapeutic, then, by all means, knock yourself out. But if your time is better spent on things like growing your business (or counting marbles in a jar), then do yourself a favor and get some professional help. Hire. It. Out.

33 Anticipate an Audit

Though I read the letter three times, there was no mistaking the grim news: I was being summoned to the IRS for an audit. I had an instant flashback to the third grade when I was called to the principal's office. I didn't know what I had done, but it must have been something bad.

After a tense conversation with my husband, I called my accountant. "You have nothing to worry about," she assured me. "We have everything in order."

The letter indicated that I needed to bring several items including bank statements, credit card statements, the prior year's tax return, and charitable contribution receipts. To my great surprise (and relief), my accountant informed me that she kept copies of all of my statements. I had them, too, but mine weren't exactly in good order. I subscribe to the "shoebox" method of filing. It would have taken days or even weeks to locate everything I needed.

I put the appointment out of my mind until the day before, and then the nerves set in. I think it's human nature to fear the IRS. I kept reminding myself that there was no reason to worry, but I couldn't ignore the knot forming in my gut.

I rode to the appointment with my accountant. She said that the IRS was increasing the number of random audits it performs. She had another client who was also going through the process, and unfortunately the client was facing her third meeting with an auditor. During her first meeting the auditor discovered a rather large personal expense on her business credit card. That set off all kinds of red flags and spurred a series of meetings to further analyze her receipts.

My appointment was scheduled to last a whopping four hours. (This is standard operating procedure.) The auditor greeted us just minutes after we arrived. Much to my surprise, she didn't look like an ogre that lives under the stairs. She was a personable woman who was clearly focused on the business at hand yet not afraid to offer a friendly smile.

We sat down at the auditor's desk in a standard office cubicle in the local IRS office. She asked me a series of questions about my citizenship and related items, and then launched into the spot-checking process. With my 2005 tax return in front of her, she asked to see a detailed report of expenses. My accountant handed over a print-out from QuickBooks.

As the auditor reviewed the details, she would periodically point to an expense and ask to see it on the associated credit card statement. My accountant had all of my statements filed by date in a binder so she was able to quickly flip through and point at each line item when asked. This impressed the auditor, and she commented that she wished more clients came as prepared for these meetings.

After about an hour of spot-checking and answering questions about charitable contributions, the auditor announced that she would not make any adjustments to my returns. She said that I would receive a letter stating the same and that I was cleared to go home.

Assume They Have Your Number

The reality is that the IRS is increasing its number of "random" audits on small businesses. Red flags can set you off in the system like extreme increases or decreases in revenues or expenses, large charitable contributions, and extensive business travel. Sole proprietors are also at higher risk of being summoned than businesses that are incorporated.

If you're ever faced with the same fate, here are some things you can do to prepare:

> Keep your business and personal finances completely separate. Using separate bank accounts and separate credit cards will keep things clean.

> It can actually be beneficial to charge most of your business expenses to a credit card and then pay off the balance each month. This way you have an organized record of your business expenses.

> Keep your accounting practices consistent. During the spot-check process, the IRS is looking for patterns. If you're asked to show an expense and it turns out that it's for a personal item, you can count on having to dig even deeper into your records. But if you show a consistent pattern with your expenses, there won't be reason to require further investigation. For example, if you travel an average of 150 miles each month for business, then a month in which you claim 700 miles will get attention. Make sure you can justify such a dramatic difference.

> New regulations require receipts for all charitable donations—even for the $10 you drop in the Salvation Army's collection can during the holidays.

> If you donate goods such as furniture or clothing, your receipt must state "Received in good condition." Not all charities are following this policy, so make sure you ask, because ultimately it's your responsibility.

> You are only allowed to place a reasonable resale value on items that you donate. The IRS agent suggested that it's best to consider what the item would sell for at a garage sale. She also uses a chart of prices provided by the Salvation Army, which you can access on the Web site (*www.salvationarmyusa.org*).

> Ask your accountant or bookkeeper about what records she keeps. Ideally she will keep copies of all of your statements in an orderly fashion.

> If your accountant isn't doing it for you, make sure your records are in order. Statements should be filed together by year either in a folder or a binder. This will save a tremendous amount of time if you get the audit call.

One last bit of advice: Don't sweat it. This may be easier said than done, but if you're following the law and keeping good records, there is no reason to fear an IRS audit. And even if this is the case and the auditor finds an error, consider the worst case scenario. Unless your error amounts to tens of thousands of dollars (which is unlikely), in most cases minor errors will simply mean that you owe some additional money. And an error could also be in your favor—you could end up getting some money back!

34 Improve Cash Flow

Cash is king in business, yet even highly profitable companies struggle with keeping enough cash in the bank. For advice on managing cash flow, I turned to Denise O'Berry, author of *Small Business Cash Flow: Strategies for Making Your Business A Financial Success.* She offered up the following suggestions:

1. **Understand how cash works in your business.** Know that profit does not equal cash flow, because assets and liabilities play a big part in your bottom line. Cash is what's left over from your profit after you've paid all your bills.

2. **Don't sell yourself short.** Make sure you charge the best price for what you offer. Consider value-based pricing and packaged services to get what you deserve. Resist an hourly fee structure; it's a dead-end road. You should charge just the right price for what your target market will tolerate. Don't be afraid to test the limits.

3. **Remember: You are not a bank.** Do the best you can to create a payment structure that provides your business with the cash it needs to operate. Don't let your invoices become idle or your accounts receivable grow. You must have money coming into your business to survive.

4. **Save cash for a rainy day.** It's tempting to go out and make a big purchase when you collect a large amount of money that you worked so hard for. Don't do it. Mantain a cash cushion in your business to help you through the valleys. Every business has them.

5. **Prepare (and use) a cash-flow budget.** A budget is the financial road map for your business and will help guide your business decision making. It should project out at least six months to give you time to plan, react to, and accommodate conditions that impact your business so you can adjust accordingly.

35 Spend It to Make It (ROI)

Many business owners don't like to part with their money and with good reason. The constant barrage of vendors who want a piece of your cash pie can cause you to cling tightly to your money. But have you ever considered that you could be missing opportunities to invest in your business and turn some of that valuable cash into even more cash?

It's called *return on investment (ROI),* and big corporations go to great lengths to evaluate the ROI of large expenditures such as technology purchases and real estate transactions. But for small business owners who are worried about cash flow, ROI can be an important consideration when parting with just a few hundred dollars.

Marketing and Advertising

The cost of advertising is one area where ROI should always be considered. Some business owners view advertising as a business *expense,* when it should be viewed as an *investment* in your business. When done right, the dollars spent on spreading the word about your business should come back to you. Though it doesn't make sense to spend thousands on an ad that will only generate a few hundred dollars in sales, it does make sense to narrow the focus of your efforts and spend what you know you can earn back.

For example, if you spent $100 on a classified ad in a publication that reaches your target customer base and your average customer spends $35, you need only three sales generated from the ad to make it pay for the investment. And don't forget about repeat business. If you an analyze the lifetime value of a client—what they spend with you on average—then you can probably afford an even bigger investment in acquiring each client.

So if you send a direct mail campaign that costs $1,000 and your average new client generates $500 in revenues, then you need just two new clients to make it worth your while.

Business Associations and Networking

Trade associations are another overlooked investment opportunity. Let's say your local chamber of commerce charges

$250 per year. This may seem steep but you will likely earn that money back. By participating in networking events, you could develop strategic partnerships with other business owners that could pay your membership investment ten times over.

Also consider the other benefits that come with membership. If chamber members receive a 20-percent discount off office supplies, and you spend $2,000 per year on supplies, you could save $400 on supplies alone. Many associations offer member discounts on a variety of products and services such as insurance, copying and printing services, shipping services, and industry-specific products. When considering joining an association, be sure to evaluate the benefits and opportunity to save. You could find that your membership dues are actually a bargain.

Education

Books, information products, and industry training classes provide additional opportunities to invest in your business. If you spend $20 on a book, even if you only learn one new strategy from reading it, that strategy could potentially help you earn thousands in the long run.

Have you ever spent hours struggling with a software program that you didn't fully understand? Investing in a three-hour class could potentially save you countless hours of wasted time—hours that could be used to generate revenues!

Outsourcing

Speaking of hours, consider what your time is worth. If you earn $100 per hour for consulting, and you spend five hours per week working on paperwork, you're essentially spending $500 a week—or $2,000 per month—on a task that removes focus from your business. Instead you could hire a Virtual Assistant or part-time employee to handle your paperwork for you. If you hired someone for less than $500 per week, you could free up your time to focus on generating new business.

Business Image

Many small businesses cut corners by trying to do everything in house. As a result, the professional image can be compromised. For example, an unattractive Website can actually detract business if it lacks professionalism, if the content has grammatical errors, or if the site isn't drawing traffic from search engines. A Web designer, copywriter, and search engine optimization expert could transform a Website from an ineffective online brochure into a money-making machine!

The next time you're faced with a business expense, instead of viewing it as another obligation, look at the opportunity. Ask yourself the following questions:

- ❧ What is my time worth?
- ❧ Will this investment save me valuable time?
- ❧ Can I generate enough sales to pay for the investment?
- ❧ Can I generate MORE sales as a result of this investment?
- ❧ Are there benefits such as discounts on products and services that will pay for the investment?
- ❧ What hidden benefits are involved? Will I be able to take advantage of networking opportunities, get valuable exposure for my business or generate business leads?

Sometimes we have to loosen up the purse strings in order to fill it with even more cash. By evaluating each opportunity to invest in your business, you can reap some tremendous rewards.

 36 Collect Debts

If your accounts receivables are inflated or you simply want to boost cash flow by getting paid in a timely manner, there are actions you can take. Michelle Dunn, author of several books and founder of *Credit-and-Collections.com,* shares the following tips for collecting money that you're owed:

1. Get paid at the time of service.

2. Invoice customers on a regular basis and as soon as the work is complete.

3. Make sure your invoices have the due date clearly visible.

4. Change your payment terms. If your terms are net 60 or net 45, change them to net 30 or net 15.

5. Offer an early payment discount to anyone who pays early, such as 1 percent or 2 percent off the bill if they pay within 10 days.

6. Act early. When an account reaches 30 days, take action.

7. Call big accounts or accounts with large balances 10 days BEFORE the invoice is due to make sure they have the invoice, that they have the correct address to send the check, that there are no problems, and that it is scheduled to be paid.

8. Be as flexible as you can with payment plans.

9. When setting up payment plans remember that you want as much as you can get as frequently as you can get it.

10. Be picky about new customers.

11. Have a strong contract.

12. Run weekly accounts receivable reports and follow up with any accounts that are past due or becoming past due.

13. Don't extend credit blindly.

14. If businesses owes you money, visit them. If it is a restaurant, go there for lunch; if it is a printing company, get something printed or copied. Every time you walk in, they will see you, and it reminds them that they owe you money.

15. Have the salesperson who made the sale collect the money or withhold their commission until the bill is paid.

16. Reduce minimum orders; you could possibly get more orders for less money paid up front.

17. Use a collection agency.

Don't Let a Mole Hill Turn Into a Mountain

Problems can happen to any business at any time.

Whether from an unexpected turn in the economy, new competition in the marketplace, or unforeseen errors within the company, before you know it, you could be faced with some difficult challenges.

Gene Pepper, author of *How to Save Your Business and Make it Grow in Tough Times,* has more than 30 years' experience as a business turnaround consultant in southern California. Pepper says that there are early warning signs to watch for that can indicate trouble ahead: "If sales are declining beyond what they should decline and there's no reason for it other than a new competitor has moved in, or your gross percentage is going down, then it's clear that the warning signs are staring right at you."

If a time comes when you see trouble on the horizon, Pepper urges you to deal with it sooner rather than later. Following are steps to take.

Vendors

If cash flow is tight and your vendors aren't getting paid on time, start making some difficult phone calls. "Tell them the truth, that you are behind," says Pepper. He advises taking a bill and dividing into six or 12 months, and then making payments accordingly. "Tell the vendor, 'We owe you X dollars. I would like to pay that over six months (or a year). Whatever you ship to us from here on out, we'll pay you COD,'" says Pepper. "This will work almost 100 percent of the time."

Employees

Pepper advises evaluating your employees' performance and grading them with A, B, or C. "Decide what each employee means to your company. A salesperson who brings in orders on time and doesn't cut prices, that's a grade A. Grade C employees should be laid off immediately," says Pepper. "They add nothing and are a constant drain on every other employee. Grade C employees are the ones who are constantly late, don't work with the team, and complain about everything."

Pepper strongly advises talking to a labor attorney before you let anyone go so that you don't create even bigger problems down the road.

Finances

The owner needs to take control over finances. "Get a cash balance every day so you know how much you have in the bank. You also need to see every expenditure that goes out, and you need to sign every check," says Pepper. Sometimes owners are resistant to taking this on, but it is critically important when the company is in crisis.

Also, run a daily aging report for your accounts receivable. "For anything over 30 days, make sure somebody is on the phone collecting the money that is owed to you."

Costs of Goods

"Make sure you know what everything costs," says Pepper. For example, if you manufacture widgets, you should know what it costs to produce each widget. Your costs may have gone up and that hasn't been reflected in your pricing. This is an often overlooked problem in struggling companies. "I've never seen a manufacturer in trouble who knew what their costs were," says Pepper.

Damage Control

"Executives need to go see customers immediately," says Pepper. "Typically senior management never sees their customers. They rely on feedback from the salespeople on the accounts. The results are tangible and astonishing from the customer's point of view." This is an opportunity for executives to connect with customers, put concerns at ease, and ensure they stick around. "This is not about getting orders. See them; take them to lunch; ask questions," says Pepper.

Business Plan

"I have never met an owner in trouble who had a business plan. Not one, ever," says Pepper. "They shudder and ask, 'How can you come in and talk about a plan when we're in trouble?'" Pepper believes that if they had a plan to start with, many would avoid ending up in crisis mode.

"I tell them to put a plan together. Not a big one, but a street smart plan with no more than ten pages," says Pepper. "It doesn't have to be elaborate and you can change it daily." Pepper says the plan should include a vision for the next two to three months that includes current financials, balance in the bank, accounts receivable, accounts payable, and a cash flow forecast.

Execute

Most importantly, says Pepper, you must take action. "Identify who is going to collect money and deal with vendors. Assign people to handle these tasks." Also, determine who you can get orders from in the next 30 days.

Lastly, Pepper says too many businesses fail to differentiate from the competition. He urges all of the businesses he works with to develop a unique selling proposition. "Figure out what makes you unique. How are you going to stand out?" He adds, "Whether you have a corner cigar shop or a hot dog stand, there has to be something unique about your business."

 **Success Interview**
Michael Ortner

Capterra

www.capterra.com

Year Founded:	1999
Number of Employees:	13

What does your company do?

Capterra is a Website that connects buyers and sellers of business software. Buyers are able to use any of our 200+ interactive software directories to identify and narrow all of their software options while software vendors are able to drive targeted Web traffic and generate sales leads.

Was there a specific turning point when you realized your business was moving to the next level?

In our 35th month of operation, we landed four new customers—after landing just three during the first 34 months. This allowed us to finally know that there was a real business here.

What processes or procedures have you implemented that have helped grow your company?

We have processes in place to support most of our activities, and most of these processes are supported by custom software. These include upgrading customers, bidding, maintaining content, charging credit cards, etc.

What are some of the best marketing strategies you have used to grow your company?

By focusing our marketing efforts on buyers, the vendors have followed. Online has worked much better than offline.

Are there any ways that you have leveraged the Internet to grow your business?

Our entire business is online, and most people find Capterra via search engines.

What challenges have you faced and how have you overcome them?

Lack of capital was a huge challenge, and we went into credit card debt to overcome that one. The chicken-and-egg dilemma that is inherent to any marketplace business model was a tough challenge that we met by offering free listings to vendors until our buyer audience increased to the point where we would be taken seriously.

How do you balance your work and personal life?

Prior to having a family, I was more of a workaholic. Now I limit my work hours to about 9 per day and figure out how to get everything done within those nine hours. I also try to keep it flexible. If my family needs me in the morning, then I'll simply come in the office late and stay late. I don't work weekends, keep work travel to a minimum, and will even bring my family if the business trip is longer than two days.

If you were starting over today, what would you do differently?

In some ways, everything; in other ways, nothing. Mistakes have been a part of everything we have done, but we have learned from those and made fixes along the way. Luckily, none have been fatal.

What advice do you have for other business owners?

Grow the number of employees slowly at the beginning when both risk and the need to keep expenses low are high.

Is there anything else you would like to add?

Take a personal role in hiring every person that comes on board for as long as possible. It seems so basic, but having great people goes a long way to creating success.

CHAPTER 6

"Never write an advertisement which you wouldn't want your family to read. You wouldn't tell lies to your own wife. Don't tell them to mine."

—David Ogilvy

The "M" Word

38 Embrace the Act of Marketing

Few businesses can truly grow without marketing. Marketing is what you do to let people know that your business exists and entice them to buy from you. Unfortunately, many business owners view marketing as a necessary evil. They don't enjoy the process, they view it as a great expense, or they just don't know what to do. But when you stop viewing marketing as an expense and instead realize that it is an *investment* in your business, you can begin to see the rewards.

I asked Jay Conrad Levinson, author of the best-selling series of *Guerrilla Marketing* books, to share his advice for business owners. "Without marketing, nobody is going to know you're there or how good you are," said Levinson. "It's like flossing your teeth. If you don't do it, there's going to be pain down the road. These are the two things everyone should be doing every day: flossing and marketing."

Levinson says that there are distinct differences between traditional marketing and Guerrilla Marketing. "Traditional marketing requires that you spend a lot of money. Guerrilla Marketing is based on four things: time, energy, imagination, and information. It takes very little money, if any."

Levinson also points out that the effectiveness of traditional marketing is typically measured by the increase in sales. But with Guerrilla Marketing, success is measured in profits. "Just because marketing efforts are increasing sales doesn't mean that the company isn't losing money. That's why we measure in profits, not sales."

According to Levinson, the one strategy that works for every business, large and small, is to start with a simple seven-sentence marketing plan. To create your plan, answer the following:

1. What is the purpose of my marketing efforts?
2. What benefits do my clients receive from my products and services?
3. Who is my target audience?
4. What is my niche?
5. What marketing strategies will I use?
6. What is my business identity?
7. What is my budget?

"The hardest part is committing to the plan," says Levinson. "A lot of people expect to see results right away and when they don't, they abandon the plan. It doesn't work in a hurry. You have to hang in there and stick with it."

He cites a campaign he worked on for Marlboro back in the 1970s. Levinson and his team developed a plan that included the Marlboro Man, beautiful scenic images, and infamous taglines like "Come to Marlboro country." At the time they rolled out the campaign, Marlboro was ranked the 31st brand of cigarette. After 18 months, they still weren't seeing results.

"The chairman of the board could have thrown us out, but he didn't," said Levinson. "He stuck to the plan and eventually it worked." No matter how you feel about cigarettes, the point is that Marlboro became the number-one brand and still uses many of the same marketing components today.

Marketing your business is a marathon, not a race. When you embrace the possibilities, the rewards can extraordinary.

Resource

- *Guerrilla Marketing: Easy and Inexpensive Strategies for Making Big Profits from Your Small Business* by Jay Conrad Levinson

39 Collect Ideas

Marketing and advertising pros are known to keep "swipe files." A swipe file is a place to store ads, marketing materials, and anything with a concept or idea that you find inspiring.

Although the idea of swiping someone else's work can sound sinister, it's quite the opposite. A swipe file can be a source of great inspiration. For example, you might clip an advertisement for a mouse trap because you like the use of a funny tag line or the color scheme or the way the offer is made. When it comes time to work on your next campaign, you can use these ideas to inspire how you are going to get the message across for your business.

The goal of a swipe file is *never to steal someone else's idea,* but to find inspiration for your own ideas. It has been said that there are no new ideas left in the world. We are simply putting our own unique spin on an idea that already existed. That's the point of a swipe file: to inspire creativity while you elevate your game.

Your swipe file doesn't have to be limited to marketing materials. I frequently clip out articles that I like. I might eventually cite a statistic I read in an article or I will research a concept further. Sometimes I want to dig deeper into a subject and write an article that follows on one I read.

When you view a swipe file as a creativity tool, it can unlock all kinds of new possibilities. It also gives you a place to store items that inspire you in some way so you don't lose them. Consider what kinds of items you run across that you would like to hang on to for future reference and designate a folder in your file drawer.

40 Build Brand Recognition

In a nutshell, branding is about creating an image for a company. Large companies spend huge amounts of money to build brand recognition, because a good brand can turn a company into a market leader.

When you think about fast food, what company comes to mind? McDonald's is the leader, and the golden arches are quite possibly one of the most recognizable images in America. I saw the power of this brand in action after taking my 2-year-old to McDonald's just one time. Ever since, we can't drive past any McDonald's in any town without him yelling out, "Mommy! French fries! French fries!"

Here are some examples of well-branded companies and what they represent to consumers:

- Wal-Mart: Low prices.
- Nordstrom: Luxury products.
- Kia: Affordable cars.
- Honda: Reliable cars.
- Mercedes: Luxury cars.
- Verizon: Reliable cellular service.
- T-Mobile: Inexpensive cellular service.

Some brands have become household names. When you sneeze do you ask for a tissue or a Kleenex? When your son cuts his finger, do you apply a bandage or a Band-aid? Do you search the Internet or do you Google?

Brand image is another place where companies spend a lot of time and dollars. McDonald's has the golden arches, Nike has the swoosh, and Target has its red target symbol. Color is another important element in brand identity. Starbucks owns its signature green, whereas Office Depot uses red. You can spot the blue awnings and roof tiles of an IHOP from miles away.

Ultimately the goal is to make your brand synonymous with a quality. You could strive to be the low-price leader, the provider of great customer service, the reliable solution, the trusted partner, or the luxury option. You could be known for fastest service, for biggest selection, or for being open around the clock.

Developing a real brand strategy can be a big undertaking, one that can benefit from expert assistance. There are brand experts in every city. If becoming a market leader is important in your business, whether you want to be known locally or globally, consider hiring a branding pro to help you build your strategy.

Resources

- *The 22 Immutable Laws of Branding* by Al Ries and Laura Ries
- *Made to Stick: Why Some Ideas Survive and Others Die* by Chip Heath
- *Meatball Sundae: Is Your Marketing Out of Sync?* by Seth Godin

41 Make Every Word Count

The value of good copywriting is easy to underestimate. I have seen this for years in my marketing business. Business owners will cut costs when redesigning a Website or developing a brochure by insisting they write the copy themselves. The result? Uninspired words that don't motivate the reader to take action.

Don't make this mistake! Good copy is essential in all of your sales materials: Website, flyers, advertisements, direct mail campaigns, and virtually anything that represents your business. Just because someone writes well does not mean that they write effective sales copy.

Bob Bly, author of numerous books, including *The Copywriter's Handbook,* says, "Copy is one of the four most important factors determining the sales that your marketing campaign with produce. The other three [factors] are the list, the offer, and the product."

The problem that inexperienced copywriters make is in focusing on the *features* of the product or services instead of the *benefits.* "Great copy begins with the prospect—her needs, problems, fears, concerns, worries and desires—not with the product," says Bly. When an untrained writer describes a product, it's easy to focus on the details that don't matter.

Here's an example for a washing machine:

FEATURE: Extra-large capacity

BENEFIT: Bigger basin can wash 20 pairs of jeans at once or your largest comforter. (Bonus: The reader can visually identify with the benefit!)

FEATURE: High-speed spin cycle

BENEFIT: Spins at a higher RPM so clothes require less time in the dryer, saving you time, energy, and money.

FEATURE: Energy-efficient

BENEFIT: Saves an average of $200 per year off of your energy bill.

Can you see how the appeal is different when you focus on a benefit?

Headlines

Effective headlines are also important because they are often the first thing a reader sees. Take a look at magazine covers to see how they craft evocative headlines that appeal to the emotions, needs, and wants of the reader.

Here are some sample headlines:

"How to Look Younger in 30 Days"

"10 Reasons to Invest in California Real Estate"

"Don't Wait for a Rainy Day; Get Cash Today"

"These Stocks Will Make You Rich"

"Call Within 24 Hours for Special Pricing"

"Parents Can't Afford to Ignore These Warning Signs"

"Free Download: The Secrets to a Happy Life"

"Travel in Comfort in Our Roomier Seats"

"Reduce Fine Lines and Wrinkles By 50%"

These headlines appeal to emotions. They appeal to the reader's wants and needs—they make you want to learn more.

The bottom line is that the right words inspire action. They can make the difference in attracting a new customer and landing a sale. Never underestimate the power of good copywriting.

42 Be the Opposite of Boring

I've attended my share of business networking events over the years and I'm always fascinated by the lackluster effort some people put into selling themselves. I remember one guy who announced, "I sell insurance. It's boring, I know. But if you need help with yours, give me a call." There is a guy like this at every networking function in every town. He shows up at all of the events; he has to. He has zero ability to inspire sales.

For advice on how to be remarkable, I turned to marketing guru Seth Godin, author of 10 best-selling books, including *Meatball Sundae* and *Tribes*. "Remarkable doesn't mean remarkable to you. It means remarkable to me," says Godin. "Am I going to make a remark about it? If not, then you're average, and average is for losers."

Speaking of average, a sushi restaurant opened in my neighborhood last year that served the typical fare. There were no bells and whistles. I can't even tell you if the food was good, bad, or somewhere in the middle because I never felt compelled to eat there. I never heard a single person recommend it. The place was always empty. Soon the doors were closed permanently. The most remarkable thing about it was that it managed to stay open for a whole year.

"If the marketplace isn't talking about you, there's a reason," says Godin. "If people aren't discussing your products, your services, your cause, your movement or your career, there's a reason. The reason is that you're boring. (I guess that's what boring means, right?) And you're probably boring on purpose. You have boring pricing because that's safer. You have a boring location because to do otherwise would be nuts. You have boring products because that's what the market wants."

On the flip side, another restaurant recently opened in my neighborhood, despite the fact that we are in the heart of a recession. Some might say that opening a restaurant during a time when consumers are clinging to their wallets for dear life is crazy. But Jack's Urban Eats is something special.

The location in Gold River, California, is their fifth in the Sacramento metro area. On opening day, there was a line out the door and into the parking lot. Jack's is a counter-style restaurant. You walk up and place an order for a salad, hand-tossed in front of you, and point to the fresh ingredients you want included. Or you can pick up a freshly roasted tri-tip sandwich, a side of mac and cheese, garlic fries, or Jack's signature bleu cheese fries. Everything about Jack's is a little bit different. You order it yourself; you schlep it to the table; you even fetch your own ketchup. Yet it's thriving in an economy that is leaving a path of destruction in business closures from coast to coast.

According to Godin, "If it's in a manual, if it's the accepted wisdom, if you can find it in a Dummies book, then guess what? It's boring, not remarkable. Part of what it takes to do something remarkable is to do something first and best."

eBay was launched as a platform for founder Pierre Omidyar to sell and trade Pez dispensers. It was anything but boring and became the world's largest online trading community. In the dotcom space, there are plenty of examples of remarkable companies. Google, *Amazon.com,* Facebook, YouTube, Hotmail, AOL and Twitter each have a remarkable quality.

The popularity of Apple's iPod, originally targeted toward a younger audience, quickly crossed all age barriers. It's compact, portable, and easy to use—and most importantly, it got us talking. The iPod is responsible for launching a revolution in the music industry, pushing consumers toward downloading music online. Soon, compact discs will be obsolete. My dad, a devoted music junkie who hasn't replied to an e-mail in two years because he can't remember his password, has more than 50,000 songs in his iTunes collection. I'm pretty sure he wants to be buried with his iPod.

Apple's iPhone is also highly regarded by users. With its slick touch screen and the ability to download applications that will do everything but brew your morning cappuccino, the iPhone is nothing short of remarkable. Ask anyone who owns one. They are in the midst of a love affair.

Godin asks, "If you put it on a T-shirt, would people wear it? No use being remarkable at something that people don't care about. Not *all* people, mind you, just a few. A few people insanely focused on what you do is far far better than thousands of people who might be mildly interested, right?"

That insurance guy, the one I met at a business event, sells an unremarkable product. But he could be doing it in a remarkable way. He could be funny. He could be controversial. He could be interesting.

How can your business be the opposite of boring?

43 Go Viral

To put it simply, viral marketing is something that happens when your campaign becomes contagious and people spread the word for you. A couple of years ago, a friend sent me an e-mail that was a brilliant viral marketing campaign. It was the holiday season and the message contained a long list of cookies. Each linked to the recipe on *www.NorthPole.com.* What a brilliant way to attract new site visitors!

In September 2000, TiVo launched a promotion that took off quickly. The company held an essay contest inviting contestants to explain why they were worthy of winning a free TiVo unit. They gave away 10 TiVo systems per day, bringing tremendous attention to the brand by those who won, those who told friends about the contest, and the resulting media coverage.

For advice on viral marketing, I contacted David Meerman Scott, best-selling author of *The New Rules of Marketing and PR* and the hit new book *World Wide Rave*. Here's what he provided:

A World Wide Rave is when people around the world are talking about you, your company, and your products. Whether you're located in San Francisco, Dubai, or Reykjavík, it's when global communities eagerly link to your stuff on the Web. It's when online buzz drives buyers to your virtual doorstep. And it's when tons of fans visit your Web site and your blog because they genuinely want to be there.

Of course, it's obvious as hell that in order for thousands or even millions of people to share your ideas and stories on the Web, you must make something worth sharing. But how do you do that? Here are the essential components.

Nobody cares about your products (except you). Yes, you read that right. What people do care about are themselves and ways to solve their problems. People also like to be entertained and to share in something remarkable. In order to have people talk about you and your ideas, you must resist the urge to hype your products and services. Create something interesting that will be talked about online. But don't worry—because when you're famous on the Web, people will line up to learn more and to buy what you offer!

No coercion required. For decades, organizations of all kinds have spent bucketfuls of money on advertising designed to coerce people into buying products. Free shipping! This week only,

20 percent off! New and improved! Faster than the other guys! This product-centric advertising is not how you get people talking about you. When you've got something worth sharing, people will share it—no coercion required.

Lose control. *Here's a component that scares most people silly. You've got to lose control of your "messages"; you need to make your valuable online content totally free (and freely sharable); and you must understand that a World Wide Rave is not about generating "sales leads." Yes, you can measure success, but not through business-school Return On Investment (ROI) calculators.*

Put down roots. *When I was a kid, my grandmother said, "If you want to receive a letter, you need to send a letter to someone first." Then when I was in college, my buddies said, "If you want to meet girls, you have to go where the girls are." The same thing is true in the virtual world of the Web. If you want your ideas to spread, you need to be involved in the online communities of people who actively share.*

Create triggers that encourage people to share. *When a product or service solves someone's problem or is very valuable, interesting, funny, or just plain outrageous, it's ready to be shared. To elevate your online content to the status of a World Wide Rave, you need a trigger to get people talking.*

Point the world to your (virtual) doorstep. *If you follow the Rules of the Rave as I've described them, people will talk about you. And when they do, they'll generate all sorts of online buzz that will be indexed by the search engines, all relating to what your organization is up to. Forget about data-driven search engine technologies. The better approach to drive people to your stuff via the search engines is to create a World Wide Rave. As result, your organization's Websites will quickly rise to prominence in the rankings on Google, Yahoo, and the other search engines.*

44 Be Memorable

The bulk of this book was written in a hotel room. With an active family life and a business to run, I have to make time to write. I also find that I'm most creative when I'm in a different environment.

I have a long history with hotel rooms. I traveled extensively for business during my time in the Silicon Valley, and still find myself on the road for speaking engagements and conferences. Last month I was in San Diego, and stayed at hotel that I couldn't wait to leave.

At this very moment, I am writing from the Hampton Inn, located just a few miles from my home. The Hampton Inn is Hilton's version of an express hotel. When I check in to hotels to write, I look for a deal. My needs are minimal: a clean room with Internet access; I try to spend $100 or less. The first time I checked in to this hotel, my expectations were low.

What is the most important thing you want from a hotel room? A comfortable bed. For less than $100, the Hampton Inn gives you an incredibly comfortable bed. (It rivals mine at home.) The Hampton also offers free high-speed Internet access that actually works (I was in a luxury hotel in San Francisco last month and couldn't get the Internet access to work at all), a super friendly staff, cable channels including HBO and Showtime, and a break- fast buffet complete with premium coffee. When I stay here, I feel like I'm getting a great deal.

This is memorable. This is a place I want to visit again. In the express hotel space, this is the only one I would ever visit.

There is a sushi restaurant in Orangevale, California. It's tucked inside a strip mall, sandwiched between a cigarette shop and a mattress store. The location is uninspiring and I wouldn't have even known about it, except a friend suggested we meet there for lunch. At the Blue Nami, the food is fresh and looks like a work of art on the plate. It is unexpected in the middle of strip mall.

The staff is always friendly. The chefs wave and yell out "thanks!" when you leave. It's memorable. It's a place you want to go back to again and again. And I do.

Being memorable doesn't have to require a lot of work. It involves a certain level of thought and authenticity. The management of the Hampton Inn figured out that a comfortable bed was key. This seems like an obvious choice, but hotels at all levels fail to deliver on this key element. The folks at the Blue Nami take pride in what they do and it shows. They provide a quality experience. I pass several sushi restaurants on my way to that one. I go there because it became an instant favorite.

Here are some novel ideas to chew on:

> A grocery store that gives away canvas grocery bags instead of forcing Earth-conscious customers to buy them. (Side note: These are a marketing tool for the business, because they have a logo on them.)

> A car dealership that offers free oil changes for a year with purchase of a new car.

> An insurance company that sends a box of fudge as a thank-you gift to clients each year.

> A coffee shop that provides a play area to keep kids busy while parents relax.

> A mortgage company that sends copies of your statements at tax time. (Following a re-finance, the company I used did this. It was a great time-saver because I didn't have to dig out my files.)

45 Start Networking

Getting out in the business community and networking can bring tremendous advantages to your business. However, some resist the idea of networking due to shyness, the time commitment involved, or a belief that it can't benefit their business. I would like to dispute these myths.

Anyone can show up at a meeting and pass out business cards like a card dealer in Las Vegas, but who wants to call that guy? The first secret to networking success is to help connect others. When you do this, they in turn want to help you.

Consider what happens when you meet Sue-the-caterer. She mentions that she's in need of a new accountant. You know a great accountant, Jeannine, so you give Sue her contact information. You've just made two people very happy. When either Sue or Jeannine comes across someone in need of your services, they are going to be eager to return the favor. In fact, they may even go out of their way to return the favor by looking for a way to refer someone to you.

It's All About Relationships

Instead of walking in to a networking function and thinking "what's in it for me?", view it as an opportunity to build relationships. Meeting new people provides the chance to not only land new clients, but form strategic partnerships, locate vendors for services that you need, test out your sales messaging, get known in your community, and even make some friends along the way.

Also keep in mind that networking isn't just about the people you meet while at an event. It's about the people your fellow networkers know. I participated in a local networking group where a makeup sales person connected a contractor with a million-dollar custom home project. That contractor could have easily dismissed the salesperson as having nothing to do with his industry, but he would have missed an extraordinary referral.

Structured Networking Groups

I will admit that I have a hard time relating to people who are shy, though I certainly empathize. I genuinely enjoy meeting new people. But for those who don't, I urge you to pursue networking opportunities that are more structured. Even I don't like to walk in to a room full of complete strangers and try to strike up a conversation. That is just awkward for everyone. Avoid events titled "mixers" and you will find that better opportunities await.

Formal networking groups such as Business Networking International (*BNI.com*) provide a structured environment where it's easier to get to know attendees. Meetings have an agenda, each attendee has the opportunity to stand up and give a brief explanation of his/her business, and, because there are often a large number of extroverts in the room, you should feel quite welcome.

eWomenNetwork takes a similar approach. Attendees participate in "accelerated networking events" where they are divided into groups so that each person shares what she does. Connections are abundant, and, though this is a women's organization, men are also welcome.

The Time Factor

We are all busy and attending networking functions does take time. I am not advocating attending every available function in a 30-mile radius. You have to visit groups to find out which ones are the best fit for you. Better yet, ask for referrals to groups that your peers enjoy. Ideally you want to find one or more groups that you enjoy attending on a regular basis. Showing up once isn't going to do the trick. Remember: It's about relationships. You have to keep showing up until you recognize people when you walk in the door, and they recognize you. That's when you should really see the results.

Resources

- *Meetup.com* is a resource for starting and finding local groups dedicated to everything from business networking to children's play groups and a lot of stuff in between.

- *Craigslist.org* is a popular spot to find many events in major cities around the world.
- *Never Eat Alone: And Other Secrets of Success, One Relationship at a Time* by Keith Ferrazzi and Tahl Raz
- *The 29% Solution: 52 Weekly Networking Success Strategies* by Dr. Ivan Misner and Michelle R. Donovan
- *Book Yourself Solid: The Fastest, Easiest, Most Reliable System for Getting More Clients Than You Can Handle Even if You Hate Marketing and Selling* by Michael Port

46 Give Stuff Away

In the food business, the goal is to get people hooked by giving them a taste. Once they know how good the product is, ideally they will come back for more. You don't have to be in the food industry to take these lessons to heart.

Carolyn Redendo, owner of Redendo's Pizzeria in Fountain Hills, Arizona, reported that offering donations to local businesses has been essential to her business: "We give gift cards (free slice for schools or $10 cards for auctions), free pizza parties, or a food donation.... The results have been great as we are growing our business and at the same time we have become part of the community."

Redendo doesn't just use giveaways to bring in news business. She also uses them to thank existing customers—an excellent way to build loyalty. "I try to make it a point to pass out small gifts or samples for a week or so prior to each holiday and for our yearly anniversary. This can be chocolate, samples of our food, ice pops, roses, etc., and we include a thank-you note with each," says Redendo. "They are passed out with all to-go orders and for dine-in customers as well."

Promotional products companies often give away samples of imprinted pens, note cards, and similar customized items as a way to lure in new business. These activities can bring in people who wouldn't otherwise have even known about the business.

Here are some suggestions for giveaways that can grow your business:

- A pet store could offer a free bag of cat or dog treats.

- A parts manufacturing company could send product samples to potential customers.

- Consultants can offer a free 20-minute phone consultation or assessment.

- Trainers and professional speakers can give away seats in a workshop.

- Virtually any kind of business with a good Web presence can offer a free downloadable report, e-book, or audio program.

 ## Success Interview

Brett Klasko

Phinaz Marketing, Inc. and Investors Alley Corp.

www.investorsalley.com,
www.swingtradeonline.com, www.phinaz.com

Year Founded:	1998
Business Partners:	I have 1 partner for 1 of the subsidiaries but own 100 percent of the overall company.
Number of Employees:	About 15, mostly independent contractors

What does your company do?

We are an interactive media and marketing firm focusing on sports and finance. Basically, there are two sides of the company: One side publishes financial news and analysis for individual investors and active traders, and the other side provides grassroots marketing advice and implementation to sports teams.

What led you to start your business?

At the age of 13 (and with the strong encouragement from my grandparents), I became very interested in the stock market (almost to the point of obsession). I was fascinated at how you could invest money and watch it increase or decrease instantly. I would check my portfolio throughout the day at school and would research new stock ideas as soon as I got home. I started publishing my thoughts and stock ideas on the Internet and slowly started to receive a following. At one point, I put a banner up to try to make a couple bucks for my efforts. Apparently the free hosting company did not want any banner ads and booted me. I was 14 at this point. I registered a domain name and a new company was born. I would stay up until the wee hours of the morning (on school nights) developing the site. I loved what I was doing, so it didn't feel like work.

Was there a specific turning point when you realized your business was moving to the next level?

One big turning point occurred when the free hosting company booted me (as described above) and I was forced to either give up my little hobby or take it commercial. That was the first point I started spending any money on the company.

But the biggest turning point occurred in March 2005 when I was about to graduate from Emory University. I still remember the phone call with my parents to discuss whether I should run my company full-time after school. The company was doing very well while I balanced school and CEO duties. But the company would need to grow to support me and my friend, who was going to become my first full-time employee. I ultimately decided to run the company full-time, which is one of the best decisions I've made, as the company has grown tenfold in the three years since.

What are some of the best marketing strategies you have used to grow your company?

My favorite and one of our most successful marketing campaigns was the Wallet Hunt. To promote our new service—Student Savvy—we went to college campuses around the country and hid wallets with up to $100 of cash in each. Students would register online or at our booth on campus the day of the Hunt and were given clues as to the locations of the wallets after registering. What would ensue was controlled chaos, as students at the campuses searched frantically for the wallets. (We may have been responsible for a few class absences.) I remember a couple incidents that really signaled that we had created quite a campus spectacle. The first was when a few Florida State campus buildings had signs up stating there were no wallets hidden in those particular buildings. The second was when a participant came up to our booth and complained that there were too many people already searching in the flower garden at the front gate of Emory University's campus. When a couple of us went over there, we were amazed to see at least 25–50 students frantically searching through the flowers, mistakenly convinced that there was a wallet to be found.

The Wallet Hunts were quite the viral campus marketing event. We received press in most of the campus newspapers for the colleges we visited, and our estimates are that we had as many as 15 percent of the undergrad population participate at some schools and that [more than] 40 percent of undergrads were aware of the event.

Are there any ways that you have leveraged the Internet to grow your business?

Without the Internet, the company wouldn't be where it is today. The Internet made it possible for some 14-year-old middle school student to gain a following based on his stock market comments. The rest is history.

What challenges have you faced and how have you overcome them?

My age was probably the biggest obstacle I faced—and the fact that I was in school. Until I was in college, I generally didn't reveal my age to readers (who in their right mind would take stock advice from a teenager?), writers (who would take orders from a teenager?), or clients (who would give money to a teenager?).

My parents always stressed the values of education, so the thought of leaving school to pursue my business full-time never really entered my mind. Instead I had to learn time management skills on the fly, as I was balancing high school/college and what was essentially a full-time job. Because I enjoyed what I was doing so much, it made it much easier to manage my time.

For the first three years of running the company, I didn't have a single business class to go on. At one point, I was going after some VC money and had to prepare a business plan and all sorts of financial reports. I went all over the Internet trying to find explanations and samples of things like cash flow statements, not to mention figuring out what "proforma" meant.

If you were starting over today, what would you do differently?

There are a couple things I would have changed. First, when I was still in high school, I wanted some "gray hair" help, so I turned to a local marketing consultant in my area for advice. While he gave me some great advice, I allowed him to handle contract negotiations with one of our biggest writers around whom we had developed a new service. The writer wasn't asking for much more but wanted to be rewarded for the service's rapid growth. My advisor didn't understand how vital this writer was to the service's future and took a very hardball approach with a guy who was simply asking for a small raise. He upset the writer so much that the writer just walked away. We tried to replace the writer but the service never rebounded. I should have trusted my own negotiation skills more (especially since I had a strong relationship with the writer) and not turned to someone else who didn't truly know the business.

Second, I've hired friends to help me with the business in the past, figuring my trust would outweigh any other factors. I never expected the very difficult decisions that would follow between keeping friends and growing the company. Most of the situations probably could have been prevented had I been up front with the friend earlier (at the risk of making them upset) before things really boiled up.

What advice do you have for other business owners?

One word: passion. If you want to start any type of business, you need to have a passion for what you're going to be doing. I became obsessed with the stock market and that passion carried over to my business. If you want to start a bike shop, have a passion for biking and the latest innovations in bikes. This passion will drive you to put your heart into the business, which is necessary to get through the inevitable hiccups of starting a new venture.

CHAPTER 7

"You can't build a good reputation on what you are going to do."

—Henry Ford

Visibility Strategies

47 Get Media Attention

Like it or not, we are all influenced by the media. The media is a powerhouse source for introducing information to an eager audience. When *People* magazine reviews a book, readers run out to get a copy. When a trendy accessory is featured in a top women's magazine, it is almost certain to be purchased by thousands.

The right kind of media exposure can propel a business, product, or service into a new orbit. Most authors who appear on *Oprah* can expect their books to hit number one almost instantaneously. The big talk shows and major newspapers and magazines are all ripe for taking a once-unknown commodity and introducing it to a new audience.

In 2001, Rachael Ray was giving cooking demonstrations at a specialty grocery store in New York. When the *Today Show* needed someone to fill in for a quick segment, Ray was invited on the show. The right people noticed. Soon Ray had a show on the Food Network, and in just a few short years she went on to host her own top daytime talk show, has written a series of books, publishes a magazine, and endorses countless products. That's the right kind of media exposure.

Even a mention in your hometown newspaper can make a difference. Lynn Rosenberg, CEO of Soleil Chic, a maker of designer UV umbrellas and hats in Marina del Rey, California, discovered the benefits of publicity when the local paper ran her story. Rosenberg's husband had died from skin cancer and Rosenberg developed UV products to help others protect themselves from the same fate. The article in her local paper prompted numerous phone calls and purchases.

"That gave me an idea of what print publicity could do," said Rosenberg. "I implemented a new publicity campaign and went full force to newspapers and magazines. I got myself in many magazines (national spa magazines, mostly) and the major one was *Travel & Leisure.* That led to American Express contacting me to get one of my umbrellas for the next day's *Today Show.*"

We have traditionally been taught that press releases are the way to go, and they can be effective as in the case with Rosenberg. You can submit press releases to individual media professionals, local news stations, radio stations, and so forth. The most popular site for distributing press releases is *PRWeb.com.*

Today, however, press releases aren't the only way to get noticed. You can also hire a publicist, and for businesses with big budgets this can be a viable option. But the majority of small businesses can't afford to spend thousands of dollars on retainer fees each month. I recommend trying more innovative strategies.

3 Secrets to Great PR

1. The media is always interested in topics that are timely. For example, if the evening news reports are buzzing about record unemployment numbers and you are a career coach, you could pitch them "5 Ways to Land a Job Interview Within a Week." This is timely and compelling and you are an expert on the subject matter, which makes you a perfect source.

    Holidays are a great opportunity to get attention if your business provides a logical tie-in. For example, if Valentine's Day is approaching and you are a marriage therapist, you could offer up "10 Ways to Relight Your Spouse's Fire."

There are also hundreds of lesser-known holidays, such as Take Your Dog to Work Day and National Small Business Week. A list of holidays is published each year through Chase's Calendar of Events.

2. **Your topic has to be news-worthy.** When you flip on the news, they aren't reporting on mundane topics like the sale at the local hardware store. They are reporting on stories that are interesting, controversial, funny, or unique. Take a look at the headlines on magazines at the check-out counter of your local grocery store. They feature stories that have massive appeal:

    > "How to Makeover Your Wardrobe for Less Than $100"

    > "Is Your Teenager Hanging Out with the Wrong Crowd? 7 Crucial Questions to Get the Answers You Need"

    > "Stop Aging Now! Our Experts Show You How"

    As a business owner, your job is to find something news-worthy about your business. Try writing your own captivating headline. Once you have one that fits, you're ready to start sending it out.

3. **Pitch the media directly.** One of the many great benefits of the Internet is that it makes the media so accessible. Nearly every media outlet, small or large, has a Website with instructions on how to submit a pitch. Better yet, reporters, editors, and producers are often just an e-mail away. If an e-mail address is readily available, you can simply pitch them directly.

    Keep in mind that the media needs us as much as we need them. They want interesting story ideas. Experts are often cited in reports. Just being a business owner makes you an expert in your industry. If you have additional credentials or certifications, even better. But don't be afraid to make direct contact with people in the media. Some of my best press coverage (*Business Week, LA Times*) has come from contacting reporters directly.

48 Develop a Publicity Plan

It is impossible to discuss publicity without input from Joan Stewart, founder of *www.PublicityHound.com.* Stewart is a former news editor who has spent the past several years teaching business owners how to get publicity.

"A publicity plan is a month-by-month plan that helps you keep track of publicity opportunities, both online and offline, that you can take advantage of throughout the year," says Stewart. "By knowing which special topics magazines and newspapers will be covering, you can prepare pitches for those special sections months ahead of time, contact journalists, and get a foot in the door long before other Publicity Hounds are aware of the opportunities."

Stewart says that a publicity plan is only essential for businesses that want massive amounts of publicity. "Without a plan, you're often simply REACTING to opportunities that you're suddenly aware of, often running around at the last minute trying to hunt for sources you can pitch along with your story idea," say Stewart. "If you know months ahead of time which media outlets want what, you'll be better prepared."

According to Stewart, a publicity plan should include the following:

➤ A month-by-month listing of opportunities in special sections for newspapers and magazines.

➤ When to pitch ideas related to events, products, services, or anything else you want to promote.

➤ Opportunities online and offline for promoting your expertise.

➣ A list of media you will target. These include not only traditional media but the "new media" including bloggers, ezine publishers, and the social networking sites like Twitter and Facebook.

➣ A list of story ideas you can pitch throughout the year.

Though publicity has traditionally been focused on print media, radio, and television, the Internet has changed the landscape and opened up new opportunities for businesses to get exposure. "As newspapers continue on the march toward the graveyard, online publicity is becoming more important. Many newspapers and magazines that publish print editions already have online editions. Some accept multi-media such as audio and video. Your media plan will tell you who accepts what," says Stewart.

"That means many more chances to get information about your events or whatever you're promoting at their Websites. Online publicity also includes the entire world of social media marketing. That includes posting videos to the video-sharing sites like YouTube, creating content at content-sharing sites like EzineArticles.com and Squidoo.com, and building tribes of followers at sites like Twitter and Facebook."

For additional information, Stewart offers a free weekly newsletter, tons of reports and audio downloads, and a course on building your publicity plan at *www.publicityhound.com/mediaplan.htm.*

49 Watch for Media Opportunities

In addition to contacting the media and sending press releases, you can emulate what the big PR firms do and subscribe to queries from the media. PR pro Peter Shankman launched a wildly popular and free e-mail list in 2008 called Help a Reporter Out (HARO). Three times per day, Shankman sends out a list of inquiries from media folks—writers, television and radio producers, authors, and even blog hosts—looking for sources for stories.

Each message can list dozens of interview opportunities. Queries might include things like:

> "Looking for a parenting expert to discuss 2-year-old discipline strategies."

> "Seeking items for gift bags for celebrity charity event."

> "Seeking experts on selling a business to discuss the pros and cons."

In fact, I used HARO to round up many of the people interviewed in this book! This is a credible and valuable source. When you come across a query that fits what you do, you can contact the reporter directly.

Visit *www.helpareporter.com/* to sign up for the free e-mail list.

50 Be Innovative

When I first met Allen Fahden, I knew right away that he was someone I wanted to know better. He has creativity coming out of his pores. You can practically see the wheels turning in his head as he concocts ideas. Here's one that just might inspire you too.

Allen Fahden wrote a book, *Innovation on Demand*, but he didn't have a publisher. So he took it upon himself to print 10,000 copies of his book and was left with no money to market it. In a radical departure, he decided to use his own book's methods for creating innovative ideas to develop his marketing strategy.

Opposites Create Opportunity

One of Fahden's major innovation techniques involves putting an opposite spin on what people expect. To sell his book, he first asked the question, *Where are books sold?* Answer: Bookstores.

Then he asked, *What's obvious about bookstores?* Answer: They're getting bigger and have more titles.

Finally, he asked, *What's the opposite of a huge bookstore with thousands of titles?* Answer: A smaller bookstore with only one title.

The result of this inquiry? Fahden opened a one-book bookstore in downtown Minneapolis. His theory is that, once you create your opposite idea, make everything else follow the norm. With this in mind, here's how he set up his store:

1. Big bookstores have many departments, so Fahden's one book bookstore had many departments. The store mesmerized visitors with thousands of copies of only one book, *Innovation on Demand,* in 13 different departments: Art, Architecture, Anthropology, Psychology/Self-Help, Business, Sports, Religion, Travel, Philosophy, Humor, Technology, Law, and Fiction & Literature.

2. Big bookstores have names and slogans, so Fahden called his bookstore ReadDundant: the bookstore that repeats itself over and over again redundantly, repetitively, and tautologically. His slogan proudly declared: "More books? Hey, we like the one we have."

3. Big bookstores have liberal return policies and customer service, so Fahden's had a liberal return policy. "If for any reason you are not completely satisfied with your book, it would be cheerfully exchanged for any other book in the store, your choice."

4. The store's top-10 best-sellers list featured *Innovation on Demand* in all 10 positions.

5. The cash register gave change only in rare two-dollar bills (the opposite of most money).

6. If anyone wanted a book signed by the author, they would get an extra two dollars back. "My signature devalues the book," Fahden would explain.

7. When the store had a sale, Fahden would select several copies of the book and raise the prices.

8. When doing readings in the store, Fahden removed the consonants from the book. He claimed with vowels only he could read the entire book aloud in 10 minutes.

9. You can't make this up: More than 50 percent of the books sold from the Psychology/Self-Help section.

Two days after opening, *City Business* featured ReadDundant on the front page ("New Bookstore Opens Anew"). On day four, three network TV stations featured the store on the evening news. Then came radio interviews, including NPR; major market newspaper stories, all on the front of sections; and even network television and the BBC.

Then, *People* magazine gave the bookstore a full-color page, a rare exposure to 35 million readers for a first-time author with a different way to promote. At the center of the photo was a sign that captured the personality of the one-book bookstore: "Shoplifters Welcome." Incidentally, during the store's three-year run (until they condemned the building), no books were ever stolen. But just after the *People* article, somebody stole the sign.

By using his own opposite innovation methods, Allen Fahden gained more than book sales and big publicity. His efforts resulted in speaking and consulting opportunities as well.

I view Fahden's story as a challenge. How can you do the opposite? How can you get outside the box for your industry and shake things up? How can your business end up getting profiled in *People* magazine?

51   Get Exposure From Speaking

If you want to reach a lot of people quickly, consider developing your skills as a professional speaker. There are dozens of trade organizations in every major city that need speakers for their weekly or monthly meetings. As a featured speaker, you receive instant credibility and establish yourself as an expert in your field.

George Huang, founder of Freedompreneur Coaching and Consulting in Mill Creek, Washington, retired from the practice of plastic surgery at the age of 40 and noted, "It wasn't the glamour sport that I fantasized it would be." After going nearly bankrupt in his first two years of practice, Huang turned his business around by developing processes and marketing strategies that worked. After walking away from his career in surgery, he planned to use his experience to coach entrepreneurs.

"Without a business networking or e-mail list, I decided to use one of my strengths: public speaking," said Huang. "Within 73 days of deciding to put on an introductory seminar, I created recurring revenue of $10,500 per month." Huang says he doubled that in the following year by using speaking to bring in new clients and selling consulting packages.

Jay Berkowitz, CEO of Ten Golden Rules, a search engine optimization service provider located in Boca Raton, Florida, says, "Our best strategy for finding new business leads is public speaking. I present strategies for Internet marketing and five or six people always come up after the presentation and ask about our consulting and agency services."

How to Break in to the Speaking Circuit

1. Write a brief and interesting description of your presentation and what attendees will learn.
2. Contact local trade associations *that reach your target audience* and let them know that you are available to speak.

3. Pack your presentation with useful information. *Do not make it a sales pitch for your business!* If the audience likes what you have to say, they will want to learn more about you and your business.

4. Your presentation doesn't necessarily need to be formal. Write an outline for your own reference and keep it with you while presenting so you stay on track.

5. Engage the audience by asking questions and solicit their participation.

6. Use props for visual interest.

7. Give attendees something to keep such as a single page handout with tips or a booklet. Be sure to include your company contact information.

8. Respect the time allotted. It's better to finish early than late—then you can open the floor for questions.

9. Wrap up with a compelling pitch for your business. I recommend closing with a special offer valid "Today Only!"

10. Send the event coordinator a thank-you note. You'll want to be invited back again in the future and this will help him/her remember you.

For additional value, have a product available for sale at the back of the room such as a book, workbook, or audio recording. Most organizations are happy to provide you with a display table and the ability to promote your products and services.

Public speaking is the number-one fear of Americans. If you aren't yet comfortable with this idea, but would like to challenge yourself to pursue it anyway (good for you!), consider joining a local Toastmasters group. This organization helps its members cultivate speaking skills in a supportive environment.

Once you're ready to seek out opportunities, pay attention to other speakers at events. What makes them interesting? How do they engage the audience? How do they pitch their services? Also, it's wise to prepare an interesting handout that includes your contact information. Ideally you want to provide the audience with something that they want to keep to reference later. This also gives them a way to remember you so that they can contact you in the future.

Resources

- *www.Toastmasters.com*—Local chapters are available in nearly every city and provide an opportunity to refine your public speaking skills.
- *Speak and Grow Rich* by Dottie Walters and Lilly Walters
- *Presenting to Win: The Art of Telling Your Story* by Jerry Weissman

52 Lead a Group

One way to become known as a leader in your industry is to run a group. You can start by volunteering to serve on the board of directors for an established group or trade association. Though this can equate to a substantial time commitment, the visibility can be great. In most associations the board members get a lot of exposure and are naturally viewed as leaders. Consider serving for your local chamber of commerce, a business networking group such as BNI, or an industry-specific trade association.

Another option is to start your own group. Two years ago I wanted to network with professional speakers in the Sacramento area. As a speaker myself, I thought it would be beneficial for us to know each other. After realizing that there wasn't an established group for speakers in our area, I decided to launch one on a bit of a whim.

The first meeting of the Sacramento Speakers Network was attended by four people in a local Starbucks. But we gained momentum each month, and today we are nearly 300 members strong with active monthly meetings that break attendance records month after month.

There are three main reasons why the group grew quickly:

1. **Online Visibility:** I used *www.meetup.com* to form the group. Meetup is an online platform that allows you to share meeting details, communicate with members, and recruit new members, because groups are cross-promoted within the local community.

2. **Unique Format:** Aside from the fact that we are the only group for speakers in the area, we have a "mastermind" component to the meeting. Attendees have a chance to get five minutes in the spotlight to discuss business ideas and challenges and get feedback from the rest of the group. This is a popular feature that brings people back again and again.

3. **Word-of-Mouth:** Because of the niche focus of the group and the unique format in which the meetings are run, word-of-mouth has been the biggest factor in growing the group.

Benefits of Leading a Group

I honestly had no idea what I was getting myself into when I launched the speakers group. It began as a fun experiment and morphed into a fairly large production each month. Without a doubt, the biggest benefit for me as the group leader is the visibility. I have become known throughout the Sacramento business community thanks to the buzz generated from the group. It has brought me countless new clients, speaking opportunities, and connections. It's also a lot of fun and I learn something from every event.

If you have the time and inclination, running a group can be worthwhile. Free listings in the calendar for your local newspapers and on Craigslist can help attract members. Also, ask your existing members to help with the recruiting process. They should be glad to contribute to the success of the group.

53 Publish White Papers

Typically, white papers are technically based documents that detail how something works or summarize facts. These have long been popular tools with technology companies as a way to distribute and share information, while passively marketing the business.

In 2002 the founder of *WritingWhitePapers.com,* Michael Stelzner, wrote a white paper on the subject of how to write white papers. He made his paper available for free download to anyone who signed up for his newsletter. "On the first day, 4 people registered for it. The first week, 40 people. The first month, 432, and at the end of the first year, over 4,000," says Stelzner. "[The white paper] helped me land huge clients such as Federal Express, Microsoft, and Dow Jones. It also led to a 20,000 reader newsletter, a portal, and a book. It was the best thing I have ever done."

White papers can be distributed via free download from your Website, handed out at trade events, or given to clients. They can be an excellent way to demonstrate credibility in your industry. For added mileage, announce new papers in press releases and online forums.

54 Publish Articles

Publishing articles establishes credibility in your field and can bring exposure to a broad audience. For example, a career coach could write articles about job hunting, effective interview skills, negotiating salaries, and dressing for success. A financial planner could write articles about retirement planning, investing in stocks, college funds, and rental property.

Once you write an article, add a short bio at the end—no more than a paragraph—that briefly explains who you are, along with a brief description of your business and a link to your Website. Once your article is complete, a good goal is to get as much mileage as you can from your effort. Start by making your article available for free reprint.

Many Websites operate on a limited budget and will gladly reprint articles written by experts. Start by looking for Websites that reach your target audience. From trade associations to information portals, you should be able to locate numerous places to pitch your content. Many sites will provide a page with article submission guidelines. If you can't find guidelines posted, send an e-mail to the site editor to inquire.

There are also numerous content sites that allow you to make your articles available for reprint in other people's Websites and newsletters. In exchange, anyone who posts your article must include your author bio. I make my articles available on a regular basis through sites like *www.ideamarketers.com,* *www.ezinearticles.com,* and *www.digg.com.*

Once you've mastered the art of publishing articles online, make each article available to print publications. Trade magazines and newsletters, small business journals, local newspapers, and some smaller magazines accept article reprints. In fact, some may even mail you a small check as a reprint fee!

To make contact, send the editor an e-mail with the article pasted into the body of the message along with the following note:

> *You are welcome to reprint this article provided the author bio is included.*

At least 99 percent of the time, you will never hear from them again. But that doesn't mean they didn't use your article. My articles will often appear in publications months or even a year after submission, and the only reason I find out is because I hear about it from a reader. That's just fine with me because I'm grateful for the exposure.

Whether you write for print or online publications, you can expect to generate plenty of Website traffic from your efforts. And the more articles you publish, the more your traffic and fan base will grow. You will also find that the quality of your articles will improve the more you write, so keep at it. This is an excellent opportunity for any business owner who enjoys writing and wants to demonstrate expertise in his/her field.

55 Publish Books

No matter what kind of business you are in, there is no better way to become an instant expert than by publishing a book. Better than any business card, brochure, advertisement, Website, or blog, a book is a powerful tool that will open doors and lead to tremendous business growth opportunities.

Think about it from the consumer point of view. Let's say that you want to hire a personal trainer. You interview a trainer with typical credentials. He's friendly, he says the right things, and his price is just right.

You interview a second trainer. He is also friendly and says the right things. At the end of your meeting he hands you a copy of his book, "The Healthy, Wealthy and Happy for Life Program." He even autographs it for you.

Who are you most likely going to hire? (Did I mention that the author's rate is also higher than his competitor?)

Still not convinced? Here are 10 reasons why business owners who are authors have the leading edge:

1. **Increase Your Credibility:** Writing a book demonstrates your expertise in your subject matter. It is a form of mastery that can elevate your status in the eyes of your potential clients,

peers, the media, and many other key contacts. The potential is truly unlimited.

2. **Sharpen Your Competitive Edge:** Just as in the personal trainer example, there is nothing like a book to impress prospects and close deals. Give away books like you hand out business cards and your business is sure to grow.

3. **Earn Higher Fees:** If you are a service provider, such as a consultant, coach, graphic artist, doctor, therapist, financial advisor, or other service professional, your book gives you a license to charge higher rates. It all comes back to that credibility factor. You are not just an average expert in your field; you are a published expert. Of course your rates are higher than everyone else's.

4. **Capture Hard-to-Get Appointments:** Want to speak with the CEO, the head of human resources, a political leader, or some other unreachable contact? Send them a copy of your book along with a personal note. Odds are much better that your next call will go through. "This is Annie Author calling...."

5. **Generate Referrals:** Several years ago, a family law attorney sent copies of her book to marriage therapists all over town. Because therapists were often talking to her potential clients, she took a chance that the book might make an impression. Her practice quickly became the largest of its kind in her city.

6. **Capture Media Attention:** Open any newspaper or magazine and notice how each article includes quotes and advice from experts. Most often, these quotes come from authors. Tune in to any talk radio show, the *Today Show,* or even your local news programs. Authors are constantly in the spotlight. In fact, media professionals from print, radio, and television frequently search Amazon.com for authors of books related to their needed subject matter.

7. **Get Known Online:** If you want to develop celebrity status and build a following of fans, there is no faster or more effective way to do that then by showcasing your author platform online. Share tips and resources through your Website, blog, and social networking sites like Facebook and LinkedIn. Host teleseminars and promote videos on YouTube. The Internet is an ideal place to capitalize on your author status and reach a global audience.

8. **Develop Programs That Support Your Book:** If you don't already have programs that support the theories in your book, you will want to have them available. Whether you ask them to or not, readers will call, write, and send e-mail inquiring about how to implement the strategies in your book. Consider developing coaching programs, training packages, and various products and services that compliment your subject matter.

9. **Build a Team Around Your Brand:** You can use your book as the foundation to teach others your system for doing what you do. You could develop your own certification program and recruit agents who deliver services under your brand, while they also promote your book and generate revenue for your business. For examples, check out Jay Conrad Levinson's Guerrilla Marketing Master Training program (*www.gmarketing.com*), Jim Horan's Consulting Team (*www.onepagebusinessplan.com*), or Michael Port's Book Yourself Solid Certified Coach program (*www.michaelport.com*).

10. **Schedule Speaking Engagements:** Commanding the attention of a room is a phenomenal way to grow your business. Authors are often invited to speak at trade association meetings, the local chamber of commerce, non-profit organizations, corporate functions, conferences, and events. Once you have captivated an audience, wrap up your

presentation with a special offer for consulting services, training programs, or other package offering. Also, be sure to sell and autograph copies at the back of the room.

The sky is truly the limit when it comes to leveraging your own book to grow your business. If you have ever considered putting your thoughts on paper, stop thinking and start writing. The sooner you get started, the sooner you can reap the rewards.

Resource

My company, *www.AuthorityPublishing.com*, specializes in custom book publishing for non-fiction books. The site also has numerous articles and tips for new and experienced authors.

 **Success Interview**
Milana Leshinsky
The Bliss Factor
www.TheBlissFactor.com

Year Founded:	2001
Business Partners:	2
Number of Employees:	0 (11 virtual team members/independent contractors)

What does your company do?

We help entrepreneurs create a business that fits their lifestyle through setting up automated income streams and a winning virtual support team.

Describe a typical day in your life.

Taking a morning walk with my iPod, updating my marketing plan, conducting a virtual roundtable for experts who want to grow a business, interviewing successful entrepreneurs, and answering some e-mails. I don't work for the sake of being busy, so everything I do has a meaning and a specific end result.

Was there a specific turning point when you realized your business was moving to the next level?

There were several. The first one happened when I created and organized a virtual conference for coaches. Almost 150 people paid $300 to attend it by telephone from 11 countries. My visibility skyrocketed and people started calling me the "MEGA" coach of the industry. This was also the year I hit my first $100,000 in income.

The second turning point came when I developed a business-building program and trained other people to facilitate it. That was the day I realized that I could truly focus on what I do best and let others do everything else.

Right now I am moving toward another turning point, which I am very excited about. I see so many entrepreneurs chained to their businesses working 10 to 12 hours a day unable to take even a week away to completely "unplug." I was able to build a different kind of business—the one where I do pretty much what I want, whenever I want.

Raising two children and having very limited time to work during the day made me think about my business differently, more strategically. Today I work only five hours a day from home making [more than] half-a-million dollars a year. It's hard to imagine that only eight years ago I was making $15 an hour working 9-to-5.

What I learned is that it's not how hard or long you work, but what you do that shapes up your lifestyle. I developed a very cool system that teaches entrepreneurs to focus on five specific things in their business and create a business that fits their desired life. This model allows you to generate as much as $3000 to $5000 in one hour without any exaggeration. The reason it works is because it's based on the two most important factors: cash flow and leverage. It moves you from the "time-for-money" mentality to "value-for-money" thinking. I call it the BLISS Factor, and you can get the entire BLISS model completely free at *www.theblissfactor.com.*

What processes or procedures have you implemented that have helped grow your company?

I hired a team. This is a virtual team, so all 11 people are independent contractors working from home just as I am. Each person supports me in their own way and allows me to be worry-free in my business and life.

I also developed a program—something I believe every expertise-based entrepreneur should have. The program allows me to hire other trainers and coaches to work with my clients and free up my time to create new income streams.

I have an online helpdesk, which allows me to leverage my support team to assist my prospects and customers. All the responses they send out get archived inside the helpdesk and can be accessed later as needed. This also allows me to grow my product "knowledgebase"—a database of questions and answers about each product anyone can access. This saves a lot of time and frustration, and can help a new team member get to know my products fast.

What are some of the best marketing strategies you have used to grow your company?

A big part of why I am able to work so little and generate half-a-million in revenue is having a mailing list—my very own database of prospects, customers, and loyal fans. I built a total of 40,000-name database over the last eight years mainly by doing two things: publishing articles and creating strategic alliances with other entrepreneurs.

You hear these two tactics all the time, but most people are missing some key factors. For example, a strategic alliance must be mutually beneficial. Asking someone to promote your products and paying them affiliate commission is not enough. I always look for ways to help my partners build their business—that's what people get excited about! In fact, that's why my virtual conferences have been so successful—they bring people together and each entrepreneur benefits from the venture through extreme market exposure, product sales, and list building.

Are there any ways that you have leveraged the Internet to grow your business?

My entire business is Internet-based. I started out by writing an e-book and built on it from there on. What I love about the Internet is the ability to feature each product on its own "mini-site." Many people spend thousands of dollars designing beautiful full-blown Websites only to realize that these Websites do not generate revenue—they are great for establishing credibility, but they do not make you money directly.

Mini-sites are basically one-page Websites that focus on one specific product at a time. This allows visitors to stay focused and keep reading until they make a decision to buy or leave. Any time I have a new product to sell, I start a mini-site with its own domain name and drive traffic to it directly. A mini-site is the best invention for product marketers ever!

What is most rewarding about running your business?

Knowing that I have no limit and can build my business to any size I choose is exciting to me. For now I choose to keep working from home with a virtual team, but in the future I might choose to move into an office and hire a full-time team.

I could add another live event, create a new program, or design new software and get hundreds of subscribers. The sky is the limit when you have your own business, but only if you set it up that way from the beginning. Many business owners book themselves solid and paint themselves into a corner, leaving no room for growth. That's why I am excited to bring my ideas to the entrepreneurs—I cracked the code for creating a business that works for you AND has unlimited income potential.

My kids are 9 and 14 now, and one of my most rewarding things is to be able to share my business with them. My son helped me run my recent conference and I can't wait to involve him at my future events and ventures. My daughter, even at 9, helps me come up with creative ideas for marketing my business and bringing value to my clients. I also love that my children get to see their mom be excited about every day. How many moms come home on Friday night and say, "TGIF!" and keep doing it year after year? I love Mondays as much as I love Fridays. My kids grow up knowing that loving what you do is not only "the norm" but also that they are in charge of creating this life for themselves.

What challenges have you faced and how have you overcome them?

The biggest challenge was marketing high-ticket programs. I was used to having instant gratification with quick $50–$100 product sales and didn't expect to have any problems selling my bigger programs. The biggest lesson I learned about marketing high-end programs is that people need to see it many times from different angles before making a decision. So pre-selling and visibility became crucial components of my marketing plans. The other thing was that people would easily spend up to $500 just by reading a sales letter, but before investing $2,000 into a program they needed to hear someone in person. That's when I added teleseminars to my marketing strategy and quickly was able to answer any questions and objections my prospects were having.

How do you balance your work and personal life?

My schedule is simple. I work when my kids are not around. This means 9–3 every day, with some occasional e-mail checking at night. I also leverage my time when I walk or drive by listening to my iPod and catching up on my continued education. I love watching movies with my husband, so I make sure I have a movie lined up for me at least two to three times a week. Plus, I walk with my best friend three times a week. She's also an entrepreneur and we have a blast together!

Notice that I didn't say that I have clear boundaries between business and life. Trying to create a strict line between business and life just doesn't work. Entrepreneurs can't shut their brains down, so they end up thinking about their business while having dinner with their family and feeling guilty about it. I integrate. I teach my kids about business at dinner and we talk about how some of it applies to what they're doing in school. My friend comes over for tea during lunchtime and we mastermind. Creating those blissful moments several times a week feels great and re-fills your mind with new creative ideas and breakthroughs.

If you were starting over today, what would you do differently?

I would focus immediately on the continuity income streams. One-time product sales are great but they cannot create consistent cash flow. Having monthly income from products like paid newsletters, CD-of-the-month clubs, membership Websites, or others, allows you to create peace of mind. Once you have a stable income stream from one of these automatically recurring products, you can relax and be creative. You can start and grow other income streams. I wish I would've discovered this sooner. Today I have four automatic cash flow streams, which is another huge part of my BLISS system.

What advice do you have for other business owners?

My mentor used to say, "There is one thing I am better at than anyone else in the world. I stink at everything else." These words didn't hit me until later in my business. There is something that every business owner does really well and it comes naturally. Your goal is to discover what that is, then delegate, automate, or eliminate everything else.

Part Three

Accelerate
(Kick It Into High Gear)

Chapter 8

"Success usually comes to those who are too busy to be looking for it."

—Henry David Thoreau

Close the Deal

56 Use Relationship Selling

I am a huge believer in the art of relationship selling.

I don't know about you, but an inordinate number of salespeople turn me off. When someone approaches me and goes straight for the sale, I sprint in the other direction.

A few months ago, I attended a business event and ran into someone I had met previously—an acquaintance. When he wandered over to say hello, I made the mistake of saying hello. He launched into a speech: "I'm actually working with a new company that sells XYZ products. I know you would love this for your business...." He rambled on and on while I shifted from side to side and looked for a chance to escape.

I don't even remember what product he was offering because he lost me as soon as he launched into his sales pitch. Good grief! Aside from the fact that it never occurred to him to ask me anything about my life or business, the following week I received a packet in the mail with a note attached to a DVD urging me to watch. I immediately filed it in the circular bin. How did he think this would inspire me to act?

To me, relationship selling is the only way. During my career in the Silicon Valley selling software, I couldn't imagine walking in to a meeting with anyone and not beginning the conversation by learning about him/her. I have always wanted to know my customers as people, and this genuine interest in people has served me well. This is especially important when competing for high-dollar sales.

Think about it. If you wanted to install a swimming pool in your backyard, you would probably inquire with a couple of companies. If the first salesperson showed up, surveyed your yard, and did nothing but talk about product features, you would probably be less than inspired.

If the second person showed up, asked how your day was going, engaged with your 4-year-old, complimented your landscaping, and then worked in to a sales discussion, you would be "warmed up." He would have worked his way into your good graces and helped take your guard down because he had built a rapport with you. Even if his quote came in a little higher than Mr. All-Business-No-Fun, you would quite likely be inclined to go with the person whose company you enjoyed.

For further advice on this subject, I turned to Elinor Stutz, author of *Nice Girls Do Get the Sale* and CEO of Smooth Sale, a sales training organization. Stutz provided the following guidelines on relationship selling:

1. **Your clientele buys you.**

    Credibility and trust are primarily the determining factors for whether or not you get the sale. Do your words, actions, and deeds mirror each other, and will you be there for the customer if something should go wrong after the sale?

    Most salespeople do not take these factors into account because they falsely believe their prospect wants to know the intricacies of their product or service, and will be impressed by their knowledge. Hence, the dreaded "telling-selling" comes to life. Engineers, in particular, make a huge blunder boring their prospects with minute details of how their products work. Their prospect loses interest. Ultimately all hope of gaining a sale is lost.

    The best method for establishing credibility and trust prior to a phone call or meeting is to research the Website of the intended company. Read the Website in depth in terms of:

- What is most important to the company.
- Challenges within their industry.
- How you can position your service or product to be beneficial.

When you call for an appointment and when you meet for the first time, remind them you visited their Website. This is the best first step to get your prospect engaged in an honest dialogue.

2. **Help others achieve their goals first.**

While in corporate sales, I was continually told I sold incorrectly, yet I was almost always the top producer. Why was that? I do not subscribe to the traditional telling-selling. Instead, I build relationships. I spent a lot of time up front asking questions to learn my prospects' challenges and goals (personal ones, too) and how I might best serve them.

Recognizing I had their interests at heart, all types of companies, including Fortune 100, bought from me. So in turn, they helped me to achieve my goals. I use the same technique today as an entrepreneur. I help my clients achieve their goals first and they, in turn, help me to achieve mine.

3. **Establish rapport with your clientele.**

When networking or meeting for an appointment, the next best step is to begin each conversation from the other's point of view. Always strive to get the other person to talk first. This reconfirms the three bullet points in #1.

You will hear and visibly see what is important to the other person, challenges he or she is facing, where he/she believes help is needed, and you will know how to position your service when it is your turn to talk.

When networking, I always begin with "*Tell me about your business,*" because that is the reason everyone is there and others are only too anxious to share. By listening, observing, and asking appropriate questions, I know exactly what to say so that they will then take an active interest in my business.

In order to get on the right track of straight talk, I will begin a serious appointment by asking a question such as, "*You are such a busy person; what caught your attention to invite me in today?*" I listen, and with permission I take careful notes.

4. **Treat everyone equally and with appreciation.**

Many times it is the receptionist or the quiet person who is the real decision-maker and he or she is overlooked and under-respected. The sale dies quickly.

A better approach is to treat everyone with equal respect no matter their title, dress, or demeanor. If you are to present at a formal meeting, ask how many people will be in attendance to be certain you bring enough copies for everyone. Draw every person in your meeting into the conversation by asking questions that concern them and the intended project.

Thank everyone for their help and time. Follow up with personal thank-you notes for each attendee after an appointment. Almost guaranteed that you will be a shining star!

5. **Serve your community.**

We all know bad word-of-mouth spreads more quickly than good word-of-mouth so it is imperative you help prospects and your community at large to build your business neighborhood. Your business neighborhood is not just who you know, but everyone who knows you and everyone else they know.

By transforming your skills into a community project, you will build a following of admirers. This relates back to Tip #2.

For example, on occasion, I will teach job-seekers "How to Sell Yourself on Interviews." It's very gratifying to receive e-mail that the sender got the job of their dreams due to the skills I shared.

Selling more, bigger, and better all boils down to doing your very best for the other party. You over-deliver on expectations and in return, the other party becomes part of your sales-force. They tell everyone they know just how good you are! Relationship selling expands your business exponentially.

 ## 57 Power Up Your Leads Strategy

It's time to take a hard look at the process you use to generate sales leads. Ask yourself these questions:

- ❧ Are we generating enough leads?
- ❧ Where are our leads coming from?
- ❧ How could we generate more leads?
- ❧ What strategies have been most successful?
- ❧ What strategies haven't worked and why?

Sometimes all it takes is a small shift to create big results. Matt Cooper, VP of Strategy and Operations for Accolo, Inc., a recruiting services firm, improved the bottom line big time by taking a hard look at how things were done: "We were focused on growing a large, enterprise-style sales team. Surely you're going to sell more if you have more salespeople, right?"

Upon evaluation, they realized that their sales team was focused on closing deals, not generating leads and scheduling initial meetings. "We shifted resources away from the enterprise salesperson and toward a more junior inside salesperson. Our number of meetings per week has doubled, and our selling expenses have been cut by 25 percent (thanks to more junior staff)."

Refine Your Lead Generation System

A sale begins with a lead. Leads can come from all kinds of activities including, but not limited to:

- Cold calling.
- Paid advertising.
- Your Website.
- Referrals.
- Word of mouth.
- Internet marketing.
- Speaking.
- Publishing.
- Networking.
- Direct mail.
- E-mail marketing.
- Social networking.
- Door-to-door flyers.
- Trade show displays.
- Phone directories.
- Trade directories.

If you aren't already tracking your leads, don't wait another minute to start. You need know where your leads are coming from so you can do more of what works and less of what doesn't work.

If, for example, you have been investing money in an ad campaign in your local newspaper, that ad better be paying off. Upon closer examination you might find that you actually generate more leads from business networking than you do from that expensive advertising—or you might find that the opposite is true.

The point is to develop a dependable lead-generation system so that you know the wheels are always in motion. Every business is different, but most can probably narrow it down to just a few key strategies that function like clockwork. For example, a home repair service might find that mailing postcards with a particular sales offer to a certain demographic always makes the phone ring. That's a system that is working. It's also a system that probably took some time to refine. The company may have tried numerous types of offers before finding the one that evoked a response. This is the dilemma of every business.

If you aren't generating leads steadily, it's time to get aggressive and test new strategies until you come up with a process that you can take to the bank.

58 Do a Rain Dance

The topic of client attraction and rain-making can cause some people to cringe. I personally enjoy the challenge of finding new ways to bring in clients, but I'm a little crazy that way. When the phone isn't ringing, I can't imagine sitting idle waiting for it to happen. I believe that my number-one job as a business owner is to make sure it's ringing all the time.

Ford Harding, author of *Rain Making: Attract New Clients No Matter What Your Field (2nd Edition)*, agreed to share some of his top strategies for generating new clients.

"Remember that you own this problem. Whether you employ a business developer or salesperson, and even if you have partners who should share a portion of the business attraction responsibility, you own the problem," says Harding. "New business is the life-blood of your firm. If it isn't coming in, noting that sales is someone else's responsibility will not help you generate the cash needed to keep the doors open. You cannot simply wait for others to solve the problem."

Harding recommends that business owners devote time every single day to make calls, send e-mail, and take other action related to business development. "Persistence is everything. Often, winning a new client is a matter of building a relationship and staying in front of the client until she has a need for what you do," says Harding. "If you think that the probability of any one call or e-mail turning into new business is low, you are probably right. But the cumulative probability of turning up business through many calls and e-mails grow rapidly. That is, it will *if* you maintain call discipline."

Another strategy Harding advocates is to be helpful. He says, "Listen for needs they have and what their special interests are. Ask what kinds of people they would like to meet. You will always have access to a client who perceives you as helpful."

Harding says that, although you want to focus your efforts on a target market, you should also develop an opportunity mindset. "You should turn down work that is too small or not right for you for some other reason. But, in my experience, over-targeting is as common a problem as under-targeting. You never know where the next piece of business is going to come from, as rainmaker after rainmaker has told me in interviews," says Harding. "Rainmakers are always seeing opportunity where others don't. They are helpful to others, even when there is little expectation that helping someone will provide a business return someday. And they do get a return on their efforts, sometimes from the most surprising sources."

You might also view this as karma. It has often been said that what you give comes back to you in multiple. By being persistent and giving when you have the opportunity, it's inevitable that your efforts will be rewarded.

59 Know the Competition

In the Silicon Valley, we were required to know our competition inside and out. We had to know their strengths and weaknesses in order to always be prepared with a response. It also helped when pitching a sale. I assumed my competitors were also making a pitch so I was able to proactively counter any possible objections. For example, if the competition had a lower price, I put the emphasis on quality, showcasing our product's performance and long-term value.

Though I don't obsess about competition the way I was trained to during my sales career, I know the value of keeping them on the radar. Every good salesperson must know what he or she is up against. You must know how your company or product is different or better.

If you haven't already been through this exercise, do a competitive analysis of your top three to five competitors. Here are some things to look for:

- ❧ **Company History:** When were they established? Who is running the show? What is their track record?

- ❧ **Product Comparison:** What features and benefits do they offer in comparison with yours? Where do you have an edge?

- ❧ **Service Comparison:** How is their service? Are they known for quality or slow response times? Is their service team local or in another country?

- ❧ **Price Comparison:** How do they price their products and services? Do they bundle products and services differently than you do?

- ❧ **Warranties:** Do they offer any kind of guarantees or warranties different than yours?

Once you've identified these answers, develop key talking points. If you assume your competitors are lurking and cut them off at the knees early in the process, you will be well positioned to win more battles than you lose.

60 Train Your Sales Team

Improving sales performance often begins with the team. To improve the competitive edge, big corporations invest in training for their sales departments. Small businesses can benefit from the same practice.

Sales training can come in many forms and cover a wide variety of topics depending on the needs and weaknesses of your team. Here are some topic examples to consider:

- Cold calling techniques.
- Prospect qualification.
- Lead generation.
- Networking skills.
- Deal closing strategies.

In additional to sales-related topics, don't overlook related skills such as customer service, personal productivity, project management, and computer applications training. By empowering your sales team with knowledge and new skills, they can only increase their value in your organization.

I recently learned about a local appliance repair company that provides employee training every single Friday! The company covers many of the topics mentioned here and more, and the results are evident in their highly polished staff. From the friendly and professional way in which the phones are answered to the impeccable appearance and pleasant nature of the service staff, the company's investment in training is clearly paying off.

Also note that the appliance company isn't spending money week after week on professional training programs. Much of their training is conducted in-house. Here are some training delivery options to consider:

- Shadow program where less experienced sales representatives "follow" more senior employees through sales calls.

❧ Classes led by a professional instructor/sales expert.

❧ Classes led by you or someone from your staff.

❧ Computer-based training.

❧ Self-study programs.

❧ Books you identify as required reading.

Options for sales training may be found in your local community or through online services. If budget is an issue, books about sales can provide a good foundation and get your team moving in the right direction.

Resources

* *The Sales Bible: The Ultimate Sales Resource* by Jeffrey Gitomer
* *Selling 101: What Every Sales Professional Needs to Know* by Zig Ziglar
* *Advanced Selling Strategies: The Proven System of Sales Ideas, Methods, and Techniques Used by Top Salespeople Everywhere* by Brian Tracy

61 Create Sales Processes

Because sales are integral to your business, processes assure that everything flows smoothly and that you have a consistent customer experience. Following are items to consider adding to your sales tool kit:

➤ **Qualifying Questions:** A list of questions or even a script used to determine if this is the right client for your company and how you can best work together. Ask important questions about the prospect's needs, expectations, budget, and any other factors needed to assess your ability to work together. This can also be a valuable tool for training your sales staff.

➤ **Proposal:** A professional document that includes a brief company overview with your value proposition, pricing, testimonials, and contact information. When it comes to pricing, consider offering multiple options. For example, you might offer three packages with different pricing levels. You may also want to include a Frequently Asked Questions section in your proposal to address any concerns the client may have.

➤ **Follow-Up System:** Create a consistent follow-up system so that you don't let leads disappear. If you have provided a potential client with a proposal, follow up within a few days to gauge their interest level and address any questions they may have. This is where you can turn an initial "no" answer into a "yes."

➤ **Client Welcome Packet:** Depending on the complexity of the services you offer, it may make sense to provide new clients with materials that welcome them to your company. This can include an overview of your processes, a list of key contacts, a user manual, a list of resources, or any other information that your new clients will find useful. This is also a great opportunity to set expectations and impress clients from the start.

 Success Interview
Marnie Pehrson
CES Business Consultants
www.ideamarketers.com and *www.pwgroup.com*
Year Founded: 1990
Number of Employees: 3

What does your company do?
Online publicity and article marketing.

Was there a specific turning point when you realized your business was moving to the next level?

In December 2007, when we started the Expert 360 Program, I knew we'd finally started to see the big picture of where we'd been heading all along. Everything we'd been building and working on for the previous eight years was building to this point.

What processes or procedures have you implemented that have helped grow your company?

I documented and delegated certain duties to my team to free up time for what I do best. For example, my husband, Greg, does our blogs and Facebook promotion. My daughter, Laurel, handles day-to-day site maintenance, audio production, and account updates. I have an assistant who handles PR and another one who writes articles and produces newsletters.

What are some of the best marketing strategies you have used to grow your company?

Getting heavily involved in Twitter and Facebook has broadened our exposure and brought in new clients. Of course article marketing is a huge piece of our business as well.

What challenges have you faced and how have you overcome them?

One of the most difficult lessons I had to learn was to let go and delegate. Delegating the maintenance of our database to our hosting provider was the first step. By shifting from a MS Access database to SQL, we were able to go from 10,000 articles in our database to a half a million. But I had to let go of my need to control.

Hiring my first VA was also a turning point in learning to let go and delegate. With the growth of the expert program, I've learned to delegate further. None of our growth would have happened had I not finally learned to delegate and relinquish control. I used to have ideas and intentionally not follow through on them because I didn't want to write checks my body couldn't cash, and I didn't think other people could do what I do. I was wrong!

If you were starting over today, what would you do differently?

I would have moved to SQL sooner, and I would have delegated sooner.

What advice do you have for other business owners?

Follow your intuition. Do what it takes to discover that "sweet spot" between trusting a higher power and working to make things happen. If you learn to listen and follow through on impressions, you'll waste less time and achieve better results with less effort. Trust your instincts and act upon them!

CHAPTER 9

"Opportunity is missed by most people because it is dressed in overalls and looks like work."

—Thomas A. Edison

Ramp Up Revenues

62 Fire Your Clients

Sometimes to get ahead, you have to drop the dead weight that is holding you back. That dead weight can often be found at the bottom of your client list. If you have any clients that are draining resources by being difficult, complaining too often, adding stress for your staff, under-paying for services, not paying on time, or requiring a disproportionate demand on time, consider firing them.

That's right; I said fire them. When you get rid of your bottom two percent, you not only eliminate the emotional baggage they carry, but you open up room for new, more profitable clients to come in.

Perhaps your company has changed direction since a client came on board and it no longer makes sense to maintain the relationship. Or maybe the whistle blows in alert whenever the client calls in because he puts everyone on edge. If a client isn't paying on time and doesn't show any signs of improvement, that's another red flag. Whatever the reason, you have the right to let some business go.

I know many, many business owners who have struggled with this challenge, myself included. We have excuses like "But they've been with me for so long," or "They would be lost without us." This comes down to a business decision. Difficult clients can affect employee morale and can hurt your bottom line. Is it more important to keep one client happy or to keep your company moving forward?

Part of the challenge comes from understanding who your ideal clients are and learning when to say no to a new client that is going to cause grief. Whether you turn down business up front or drop business on the back end, the point is to get clear about what constitutes a good client and how you company best serves all of its clients. Sometimes these two elements don't align and you have to have faith that better opportunities will take their place.

63 Evaluate Pricing Decisions

I have never been an advocate of being the low-price leader. Unless you are aiming to be the Wal-Mart of your industry and plan to make up for low-price sales in volume, I believe in charging what you're worth and then demonstrating the *value* to your customers.

Perceived value comes into play when you make any kind of purchase. For example, some people purchase the name-brand mayonnaise over the store brand. The store brand costs less and they assume that the quality won't be as great, so they are willing to pay extra for quality. On the other hand, there are people who prefer savings over quality and will instead opt for the store brand.

As business owners, we can choose to lead with a low price or lead with value. When I have my carpets cleaned at home, price is my last consideration. As a mom, I want my carpets to be thoroughly cleaned and free of chemicals. I am skeptical of the low-priced carpet cleaners, because I know they are working on volume and probably aren't using the highest-quality products to get the job done. Right or wrong, this is my perception.

Studies show that most people land somewhere in the middle. So when you are shopping for a new washing machine, you will probably assume that the lowest-priced machine isn't going to be as good, the highest-priced machine is more than you need, and therefore the one in the middle is going to give you the right balance of price and value. However, if that high-priced machine washes twice as many clothes and that is important to you, it could be worth paying the extra money.

If you are the maker of the high-end washing machine or any product or service that is priced on the higher end of the spectrum, it's up to you to demonstrate the value. From a business perspective, when you are on the high end of the spectrum for your industry, you need fewer sales than the business on the low end of the spectrum. For example, a copywriter who charges $50 per hour has to work four times more than the one who charges $200 per hour. But the one charging $200 probably has to work a little harder to close business and prove his/her value.

The other pricing challenge comes from knowing when it's time to raise prices. Some business owners fear that increasing prices will alienate customers—and it might. But then again, it might not. If your prices haven't increased in more than two years, take a close look. Has inflation increased? Has your cost of doing business gone up? Would you eliminate some of your difficult clients as a result? Are you able to demonstrate your value at a higher price?

A lot of factors should go in to pricing decisions: what your target market is willing to pay, what they can afford, how your business is different than the competition, how much competition you have, whether your costs have increased, and how long it's been since you last raised prices. There is no right or wrong answer for every business, but I'm suggesting that you take a closer look and consider your options. It might be time for a raise.

64 Create an Affiliate Sales Program

An affiliate program allows you to pay a commission to others who refer sales to you. This is commonly used in the land of Internet marketing. For example, a company might develop a training program that sells for $500. In order to entice others to promote it, the company will offer a substantial commission (25 to 50 percent) for any sales made as a result of a referral from an affiliate partner.

On the Internet, these programs are tracked with affiliate links. Ecommerce shopping cart programs like 1shoppingcart.com allow users to designate affiliate links and provide them to others. So when company A promotes its training program, company B receives a unique tracking link to place in a promotional e-mail. When a subscriber to company B's e-mail list clicks through to order the program, company A receives a report showing where the sale came from and can then pay the appropriate commission.

Less-formal affiliate programs are better known as referral partners. Graphic designers often participate in these programs with companies that print materials. So when a client hires a graphic designer to create a brochure, the designer will have it printed with a printer that provides him with a commission on the sale.

Another term for this is *finder's fee.* You could provide incentive to others who send business your way by offering them a percentage of the sale or a flat fee. For example, a house cleaning company might team up with carpet cleaner and provide a finders fee whenever the carpet company recommends a new client to the housekeeping company.

Sharon Armstrong, president of Sharon Armstrong and Associates, a human resources consulting firm, says, "The single best strategy I used to grow my business was to pay a small finder's fee for any lead that resulted in an assignment. I would either send a check to the colleague who told me about the opportunity, or I would write a check to their favorite charity."

Resources

- *CommissionJunction.com* and *Linkshare.com*—
  Premium affiliate programs that manage services for
  companies like Office Depot and eBay.
- *ClickBank.com*—A portal for listing and selling
  downloadable products.

65 Discover the Power of Coupons

An entire industry has evolved around promoting coupons and discounts to shoppers. Sites like *ecoupons.com,*
coolsavings.com, and *couponsurfer.com* give consumers a place
to collect discounts on everything from groceries and office supplies to furniture and travel.

Although at first glance you might see this as a way for consumers to cheat the system by effectively shopping for discounts,
it can actually be a boon to the retailers who get added exposure
from these sites.

Coupons can be a great way to bring consumers in to a business.
Risa Barash, co-owner of Fairy Tales Hair Care for Children, says
that posting coupons online has had a big impact on her business.
"We implemented a referral program on our website and within
days our existing customers sent along our coupon code to over
700 new and potential customers."

Coupons are easy to distribute, especially online. Like most
marketing campaigns, the results will come from testing what
works best to bring in new business.

66 Establish Joint Ventures

Joint ventures come in all shapes and sizes, and one
thing is for sure: they are under-utilized in business.
Teaming up with another company allows you to cross-promote
your products and services. Ideally you want to create a win-win
situation so that each business can benefit.

One local salon runs a smart promotion on Valentine's Day: "Buy a $200 Gift Certificate, Get a $50 Gift Card for Dinner." The salon teamed up with a popular restaurant to add value to the offer. Imagine what happens when a husband stops in to buy his wife a gift certificate. Instead of the $100 he was planning to spend, he will likely up the ante to $200 because he gets a bonus certificate to a top restaurant.

Years ago when I owned my bookstore, I teamed up with the drive-through coffee shop down the street. For a month we each handed out each other's coupons. Everyone who bought books received a coupon for coffee, and everyone who bought coffee received a coupon for books. This program worked like a charm for both of our businesses, bringing each of us new customers.

How can you team up with another business and help each other be successful? Could you swap ads in each other's newsletters? Offer a bonus with purchase? Co-promote each other's events? Consider the possibilities.

67 Develop Channel Partners

Much of Microsoft's success can be attributed to channel partners—businesses that bundle Microsoft's products into their own. For example, when you buy a new PC, Microsoft's operating system comes pre-loaded. For an additional fee, you can purchase Microsoft Office tools such as Word, Excel, and PowerPoint, yet you never deal directly with Microsoft.

These channel partner relationships have helped Microsoft grow into the mammoth industry leader in the PC arena. Companies like Dell and HP negotiate terms with Microsoft in order to resell their products. Not only has this strategy helped Microsoft saturate the market with its products, it minimizes the amount of direct sales the company needs to make.

Channel partnerships can work in all kinds of businesses. An independent contractor can resell custom cabinets from a local supplier. A chiropractor can provide supplements to her clients from a premium manufacturer. When a freelance writer does work for a marketing company, the company essentially becomes a channel partner, distributing the writer's content to its clients.

What kinds of companies would make good channel partners for your business? Though you may need to discount your products and services to make this relationship work, ideally you should make that up in volume. Conversely, is there another product or service that you would like to be able to offer your customers? Perhaps you can become a reseller for someone else.

68 Acquire a Company

Many of the big companies subscribe to the policy of growth-through-acquisition. There are several reasons to consider acquiring another company:

- Obtain something that is already available instead of building a new product or service.

- Knock the competition out by buying them—and their customers.

- Expand into a new market in another region.

One acquisition-happy company is Google, which has gobbled up more than 50 firms since its incorporation in 1998. Based in Mountain View, California, Google's strategy is to acquire companies that complement or add to its list of available products and services. Some of the most notable acquisitions include YouTube, a free video-sharing platform, and DoubleClick, an online advertising company that helped aid Google's domination in the Internet advertising arena.

For advice on how an acquisition can help you grow your business, I turned to Andrew Rogerson, an author of several books, including *Successfully Buy Your Business: Expert Advice from a Business Broker*. Rogerson says that there are three types of buyers: synergistic, industry, and strategic.

The synergistic buyer looks for a company with complementary products or services. "For example, if you are a coffee distributor, it could make sense to buy the largest coffee retailer in town. You can then provide the coffee to the retail business at the distributor's price and now earn the retailers mark up," says Rogerson. "Another strategy could be to buy the farm that grows the coffee. Now you can provide the full service from ground to cup and take all those profits that are part of a cup of coffee."

An industry buyer is a director competitor of the seller. "His strategy is to take out the seller so he now has a greater market share than before and in theory, now increase his price for the same service and make his combined operation more profitable," says Rogerson. "For example, the buyer may have a tire repair business and there are four in town. He knows that if he takes out one of his competitors it will give him greater market share and more profit to compete much more aggressively against the remaining competitors."

A strategic buyer is someone whose business is successful in a local or regional market. "If he buys out a business in another local or regional market he will increase his market share. With increased market share comes the ability to negotiate better prices, quality of product, terms of credit, etc., from suppliers and therefore make his business more profitable," said Rogerson.

When considering an acquisition to grow your company, Rogerson says that it comes down to leverage. "If a buyer can buy a business and put down 20 [percent] as a down payment and borrow the rest, they have the capacity to grow that 20 [percent]. The higher the down payment, the more business the buyer can buy," says Rogerson. "For example, a business that costs $500,000 requires the buyer to have 20 [percent] or $100,000 in cash. However, if the buyer has $200,000 in cash, he can buy a business worth $1,000,000."

As someone who has been through the process of selling a business, I highly recommend obtaining the services of an experienced business broker to assist you in finding the right company to buy and negotiating the transaction. This is not a place to cut corners. A broker's experience can help you uncover details you might not otherwise know about and can look out for your best interests.

 ## Success Interview
Linda Abraham
Accepted.com
www.accepted.com
Year Founded: 1994
Number of Employees: 4

What does your company do?

Admissions advising and application essay editing.

Was there a specific turning point when you realized your business was moving to the next level?

The business has continuously evolved since we launched our Website in 1996. Launching the Website then was definitely a major "a-ha" moment. I realized that the web removed geographic limitations. But since then, it has grown through experimentation and development.

If I had to mention another turning point it was probably around 2003. Application volume dived and revenue declined for the first time. I realized that I could no longer just do what

I had been doing—maintaining the Website as I had since 1998 and providing excellent service. I had to market in different ways and be open to change and constant self-education in the dynamic environment of the Internet.

What processes or procedures have you implemented that have helped grow your company?

We are a premium company and I insist on quality editing and prompt service. My editors cannot return work late.

We are attempting to apply more quantitative rigor to marketing initiatives. We test changes to the Website to see what helps us achieve our goals, as opposed to just acting based on what I or my assistant likes.

We also, about two years ago, started using a Web-based CRM program. It's not cheap, but it allows us to work more efficiently and better serve our customers.

What are some of the best marketing strategies you have used to grow your company?

❧ Providing good content and resources for free has helped me grow the business. My company demonstrates expertise and helps applicants; prospective customers have the opportunity to get comfortable with us.

❧ Answering questions in applicant forums. Again, this allows us to demonstrate expertise.

Both strategies also create trust. If we are this good for free, how much more can we help when we are paid?

Are there any ways that you have leveraged the Internet to grow your business?

Our Website and word-of-mouth are our two biggest sources of business. I advertise very little and invest a lot in the Website. I want it to be something that applicants will find beneficial. I view it as our first and best "advertisement," second only to word-of-mouth among satisfied customers.

In addition, we have invested a lot in SEO and making sure that we are found. For most of our key words, we are on the first page in Google, and Google is one of our biggest sources of traffic.

What challenges have you faced and how have you overcome them?

Balance is the largest challenge. When my children were younger, they were my top priority. Now that they are grown, I find it more difficult to tear myself away from my desk and keep family and other values appropriately on my schedule.

If you were starting over today, what would you do differently?

I "designed" my first Website, because I viewed the Website as an experiment. I would never do that today.

What advice do you have for other business owners?

Make sure you are filling a genuine need or offering a valuable service.

Strive to be the best in your market at what you consider important. If you compete on price, your prices have to be the lowest in your market. If you compete on quality, you have to do your best.

CHAPTER 10

"To solve any problem, here are three questions to ask yourself: First, what could I do? Second, what could I read? And third, who could I ask?"

—Jim Rohn

Get Cyber-Savvy

69 Optimize for the Search Engines

Search engine optimization, also known as SEO, is a process used to help your Website achieve top rankings on the search engines when someone searches for your products or services. Google, the leading search engine with 70 percent of search traffic, and Yahoo!, a distant second in search traffic, use complex algorithms to rank the relevance of each Website.

Google uses technology known as "spiders" that "crawl" Websites to evaluate patterns. Among many factors analyzed, the spiders look for keywords and phrases. For example, if your company sells used musical instruments in Seattle, your site should reference "used musical instruments" and "Seattle." In fact, keywords are the very core of search engine optimization. Each page of your site should have its own keyword/key phrase strategy.

For your home page, the key phrase might be "used musical instruments in Seattle." You might also add additional pages for used guitars, used drum sets, used clarinets, and so forth. For maximum SEO impact, the keyword phrase for each page should be included in the meta tags, title, and description, and repeated several times within the text on the page.

Jay Berkowitz, CEO of Ten Golden Rules, a provider of search engine optimization services, uses SEO strategies for his own company: "We come up on the first page of Google for many searches such as 'Florida marketing consultant' or 'Florida consulting interactive marketing.'"

Here are some additional SEO tips:

➤ Use long-tail keywords within your site. This is when you embed a Web link into words on a page. Instead of simply saying "Click Here," a link should indicate what kind of content the link is pointing to such as "How to Clean a Flute."

➤ Whenever possible, use long-tail keywords with incoming links to describe your site. For example, if you belong to a trade association that provides you with an online profile, see if you can use a phrase like "used musical equipment in Seattle" instead of simply listing your Website.

➤ Add a site map to your site's home page. This is simply a directory of links to all the pages within your site. This helps the search engines easily locate and crawl all pages.

➤ Update content frequently. One of the worst things you can do is let your site sit idle without adding or changing information. Ideally you should add or update content several times each week. If your site has been sitting idle for months, it is hurting your search engine relevance.

➤ Add tags to all images on your site. You have the ability to embed keywords and phrases into pictures for additional exposure. Never let an image sit without taking advantage of keywords.

➤ Avoid the use of flash on your site. Flash is the fancy animation that can look nice on a site, but can actually block the search engines from being able to read your content.

➤ Add more content to your site in the form of articles, resources, industry news, case studies, and so forth. The more content you have, the more reasons you give the search engines to find your site. For example, an article on "How to Restring a Guitar" might bring in new customers who wouldn't have otherwise found your site.

"Another tactic that is amazing is Web-optimized press releases. This combines PR and search engine optimization to build press releases around key phrases you want to feature in Google and the other search engines," says Berkowitz. "Our press releases get picked up in searches for phrases such as 'keynote marketing presentation.'"

Keywords aren't the only factor in good SEO. The search engines also look for Web links pointing to your site from other relevant sites. The used music store might have links coming in from music schools and music industry associations. This will increase the relevance factor and add credibility to your site.

Good SEO can make the difference between a site that receives a few visitors a day and a site that receives hundreds and even thousands of visitors. For assistance, seek out a service that can help. You can also do a lot of the work yourself using strategies outlined in books and online.

Resources

- *Search Engine Optimization: Your Visual Blueprint for Effective Internet Marketing* by Kristopher B. Jones
- *Search Engine Optimization: An Hour a Day* by Jennifer Grappone and Gradiva Couzin

70 Pay to Play

In simple terms, pay-per-click advertising allows you to bid on keywords and phrases in order to have your site listed in the top of the search results with the major search engines. The cost per click is based on the popularity of the search term and how many other advertisers are bidding for placement. Bids can start as low as $.15 per click for less-popular search terms and can run as high as several dollars each for popular phrases.

Google AdWords (*adwords.google.com*) is the top option for paid search engine advertising. Google can also place your ad and Web link on other Websites based on keywords you specify. For example, if you run an ad campaign for a fancy kitchen gadget, your ad would likely be placed on cooking-related sites. Yahoo! is the second most popular search engine and also offers pay-per-click advertising options (*sem.smallbusiness.yahoo.com*). Both Google and Yahoo! allow you to specify a variety of demographic criteria such as location and income level.

The challenge with pay-per-click ads is that you are paying *only for a click through to your site,* not when you've actually sold something or gained a new customer. The costs for these services can add up quickly. You do have the option to set a budget so that if you're only willing to spend $100 per month, your ads will be temporarily suspended once you've reached your budget limit and will start again the next month.

However, if you have a niche topic or want to drive traffic to your Website, it may be worthwhile to test the pay-per-click advertising model. With some testing of different keyword combinations and persuasive ad copy, this strategy has the ability to draw traffic quickly.

Michael Browning, Director of Strategic Development for Chapman Kelly, a health insurance agency, credits Google Adwords for boosting business big time. "In less thank six months, we drove traffic up more than 1,000 percent and increased our website leads from 0 to over 35 percent of our incoming proposal requests," says Browning. "We were recently named the sixth-fastest growing business in the Louisville, Kentucky, area by Business First Louisville." This was all accomplished in-house after reading *The Ultimate Guide to Google Adwords* by Perry Marshall and Bryan Todd.

Keep in mind that you can draw the best traffic in the world, but, if you're not converting that traffic to sales, then you may need to tweak your ad or the landing page on your site. If users are visiting but not buying, the offer may not be strong enough or you may not be qualifying the visitor with the ad copy. Be as specific as you can in your ad so that you pull in real leads. Misleading ads will be expensive and wasteful.

71 Profit From Information

Information products such as books, e-books, special reports, teleseminars, podcasts, videos, workbooks, tips booklets, and virtually any method in which you can deliver information, can become lucrative revenue streams for many kinds of businesses.

The most important element of a good information product is that it must teach buyers how to do something. Here are some examples:

- An interior decorator could produce a video demonstration showing how to design a fashionable home.

- A garden center could sell how-to videos of various gardening techniques.

- A successful freelance professional in virtually any industry could develop products that teach other freelancers how to emulate their success.

- A nutritionist could develop a workbook-style food journal that includes a menu of safe foods for people with food allergies or other health issues.

- A professional organizer could sell admission to teleclasses (held via conference call) and teach everything from organizing your office to preparing for a new baby.

Keys to Info Product Success

In order to convince customers to get out the credit card and make a purchase, you need to follow a basic formula for success:

➤ **Credibility:** Demonstrate any credentials that you have in your field. This is not the time to be shy. Publicize your education, experience, awards, or achievements in the area that you specialize. Strangers are not going to buy from you unless you can demonstrate your ability to deliver on your promises.

➤ **Quality:** There are plenty of information products out there, and some are downright lousy. Make sure that whatever you produce is of the highest quality. All products should be professionally produced and edited.

➤ **Value:** There is a fine balance when determining the price of products. Too many infopreneurs price their products out of the ballpark. Check to see how your competitors are pricing their products. Some price products higher to demonstrate the extreme value of the information they are selling. If you use this strategy, be sure you are delivering information that is worth its weight at checkout.

➤ **Delivery:** With electronic products such as e-books and re-ports, customers who purchase want instant gratification. Though you can manually e-mail electronic products once a sale is completed, it's best to automate the delivery process. An added advantage of automation is that you won't have to con-stantly check e-mail for sales notifications, and you can actually make money and deliver products while you sleep. A good ecommerce shopping cart system such as *1shoppingcart.com, payloadz.com,* or *practicepaysolutions.com* will get you up and running.

Checklist for Information Product Success

___Product and service offerings meet a need in the marketplace.

___ Defined target audience who can afford your offerings.

___Sales copy details benefits for buyers and inspires readers to take action.

___Website provides an easy online ordering process.

___A multi-pronged strategy for generating website traffic (pay-per-click, strategic partnerships, search engine optimization, article submissions, advertisements, etc.).

___High-quality products and services. (If the quality is missing, you will never be able to leverage valuable repeat business.)

___Big picture strategy with both short-term and long-term goals.

___Ongoing marketing strategy to continue building sales.

___Pay-per-click ads. (They can work well for some niche products.)

Resources

I wrote an entire book on this subject: *From Entrepreneur to Infopreneur: Make Money with Books, e-Books and Information Products.* Free resources are also available at *www.businessinfoguide.com/infopreneur.htm.*

72 Market With Information

Information can be delivered in a variety of formats, including books, e-books, special reports, booklets, workbooks, newsletters, articles, teleseminars, and workshops. As discussed in the previous section, information can be turned into revenue-generating products. You can also use information products as a powerful marketing tool for your business.

When marketing with information products, the goal is to provide useful information that will inspire the recipient to want to learn more about your business. Unlike brochures and other marketing collateral, information products with practical information are more likely to be kept around and referenced over and over again.

Michael Tasner, CEO of Taz Solutions, a Web design services company in Niagra Falls, New York, says education-based marketing has been essential in growing his business: "When we started we were very 'us' centric in our marketing. Getting the sale was our only concern so we could grow the company and continue to stay cash flow-positive. Then it hit us. We needed to stop focusing on us and start focusing on our prospects and customers."

"When you are totally focused on helping others get what they want, your sales start to increase naturally and things start happening with much more ease. Our key strategy focused on helping others was to practice education-based marketing and selling," said Tasner. "We published a blog chock full of great content that we normally would keep secret. We wrote and gave away 14 different free white papers and even gave our list of places we leverage to increase our customers' traffic and sales. At first we were concerned that people would run with the free information (and some did), but most came back to us for an engagement!"

Following are some examples of ways information can be used as a marketing tool:

> A career coach could send prospects a special report called "How to Speed Up Your Job Search."

> An accountant could send clients an e-book called "The Ultimate Tax Planner" with instructions and checklists that clients use to gather up the required paperwork for filing annual taxes. Not only would clients appreciate this valuable resource, but it would save hundreds of dollars compared to the costs of printing and shipping similar information.

> A business consultant could create a workbook called "Take This Job and Shove It" and include strategies and processes for writing a business plan and developing a corporate exit strategy.

➤ A personal trainer could create a workbook called "30 Days to Better Health" that includes diet and fitness tips along with a journal component that allows clients to track their progress.

➤ A home cleaning business could host a free teleseminar on "25 Ways to Reduce Allergens in Your Home."

➤ A real estate agent could create a booklet called "Essential Local Resources" that includes a list of contact information for people moving into new homes, such as local pizza delivery, the chamber of commerce, pet-sitting services, carpet cleaning services, and so on.

➤ A day spa could create a video called "How to Get the Salon Look at Home" that offers skincare tips and upkeep information for new hairstyles.

73 Create an eCommerce Strategy

If you are in the business of selling products and/or services, and you're not making them available through your Website, there is a good chance you're losing money. The Internet allows us to reach potential customers around the globe.

Allow me to share an example. When my dad's birthday was approaching last year, I decided to get him a gift certificate to his favorite golf course. I located the site and began looking for the online store. All I found was a phone number to the pro shop. Perplexed and mildly annoyed by the inconvenience, I picked up the old-fashioned phone and dialed. "I'd like to purchase a gift certificate, but I can't find the link on your site."

"That's because there isn't one," replied the pro shop guy.

"Well then, can I place an order with you now?" I asked, credit card in hand.

"Nope, sorry. You have to come in to the pro shop."

"But I live two hours away. I really can't place an order online *or* over the phone?"

Seriously? I still can't get over this one. Every business should have this ability, even if just for gift certificate sales. Not having these available online equates to LOST REVENUE! (Incidentally, that pro shop could be selling some of its products online, too.)

The good news is that it doesn't have to be difficult to implement ecommerce solutions. Online shopping-cart technology and credit card processing is easier than ever to employ. Following is a look at some of your choices.

Paypal

If you have a limited number of products or you simply want to test the waters, Paypal provides a quick and easy way to add a shopping cart to your Website. This wholly owned subsidiary of eBay is primarily a payment processing service. Once you sign up for a free Paypal account, you can quickly create shopping cart buttons to insert on your Website.

When a customer makes a purchase, Paypal takes the buyer through the payment process and delivers an e-mail receipt when payment is complete. As the merchant, you receive notification via e-mail that your product has sold, along with the buyer's shipping information.

Like all merchant card processors, Paypal charges a fee per transaction. Paypal used to require shoppers to register with the payment service before it would process an order, but this is no longer the case. Today orders processed through Paypal are comparable to many other online shopping experiences. For additional information, visit *www.paypal.com*.

Google Checkout

In an effort to compete with Paypal and leverage its mammoth Internet power, Google launched its own payment processing service. Google Checkout allows you to create a shopping cart or integrate Google services with your existing shopping cart. Google reports that more users click on items that are advertised with a Google Checkout button. For additional information, visit *checkout.google.com/seller/.*

Amazon Payments

Not to be outdone, Amazon.com also offers a suite of ecommerce solutions. Checkout by Amazon provides shopping cart solutions that you can integrate with your site, including Amazon's popular 1-Click checkout. Amazon Simple Pay allows users to use their payment information from their Amazon.com account to pay you for products and services. For additional information, visit *payments.amazon.com/sdui/sdui/home.*

1ShoppingCart.com

If you intend to sell a large volume of products, 1ShoppingCart provides a comprehensive shopping cart solution. Depending on the level of service you choose, you can create shopping cart buttons, offer special discounts or sale prices on your products, create gift certificates, launch an affiliate program and pay others a commission for selling your products, automate e-mail delivery with auto-responders, and even deliver e-books securely.

You can also use 1ShoppingCart's merchant account provider to process credit cards or integrate the shopping cart with your existing merchant processor (providing they are an approved provider). Separate transaction and monthly fees apply so be sure to check the website for the latest fee schedule. For additional information, visit *www.1shoppingcart.com.*

Payloadz.com

If you're selling electronic downloads such as e-books or mp3 files, Payloadz allows you to set up shopping cart buttons and automates the delivery of your electronic products. The service is integrated with Paypal, so payment transactions are easily processed through your Paypal account. For additional information, visit *payloadz.com.*

Yahoo!

If you would like to create a custom online store, Yahoo! Merchant Solutions may be the answer. Merchants with Yahoo! are listed in their directory of stores for added exposure.

Yahoo! stores integrate with most merchant card processors or you can sign up for an account with one of their partners. Yahoo also offers incentives for signing up such as credits toward search engine marketing services and discounts on services from their partners. For additional information, visit *smallbusiness.yahoo.com/merchant.*

✸ 74 Generate Big Money From E-mail Marketing

When people sign up for your mailing list, they are granting you permission to market to them. Talk about a powerful opportunity! It is the goal of virtually every major retailer, and many service providers to develop a substantial e-mail list because that list generates dollars.

Here are some benefits:

➤ **Saves Money:** Direct mail and print ads are expensive and often have a low return on investment. Electronic newsletters cost far less and can be significantly more effective. According to *emaillabs.com*, the return on investment (ROI) for e-mail is astounding: $51.45 for every $1 spent. Compare that to non-Internet marketing ROI of $21.08.

> **Proven Response Rate:** With direct mail (a sales letter or other printed item sent via postal mail), you are lucky if you get a 5-percent response rate. The industry average for e-mail marketing is a 25 percent. Plus, the right marketing software will allow you track how many people opened your messages, clicked through to your website, and more.

> **Promotes Your Business With Existing Customers:** It costs far less to up-sell to existing customers than it costs to acquire new customers. A newsletter allows you to maintain communications with your customer base and promote your products and services on an ongoing basis.

> **Shortens Sales Cycles:** An old marketing adage indicates that consumers must be exposed to a product an average of six to eight times before making a decision to buy. An electronic newsletter allows you to get repeat exposure with your prospects and customers on a regular basis, ultimately improving your sales process and shortening sales cycles.

> **Builds Customer Loyalty:** Studies show that an effective newsletter can bond the reader with the company, especially in organizations that cater to enthusiasts such as wine shops, fitness centers, life coaching, art galleries, and religious organizations. By providing quality content in your electronic newsletter, you add value for your customers and build loyalty that can last a lifetime.

> **Improves Professional Image:** A professional newsletter elevates your business image and gives you an edge over the competition.

> **Creates Immediate Results:** E-mail marketing is timely. You can publicize events, promote new products and services, and announce special sales. A strong call to action along with a special offer, discount, or sale gives newsletter readers incentive to make an immediate purchase.

Keys to Success

1. Send your campaigns or e-newsletter at regular intervals (for example, the second Tuesday each month or the first and third Friday each month). Your readers will appreciate that it is predictable.

2. Studies show that your heading should be less than 50 characters. Make it engaging so you can prompt readers to open the message. Readers also tend to react when their name is in the subject so use software that allows you to include first names.

3. Many e-mail users now read messages with preview panes. That means that the first few paragraphs of your campaign should be engaging in order to convince the recipient to keep reading.

4. Use a table of contents to entice readers. Better yet, make the subjects clickable so it's easy to navigate your message.

5. Include a good balance of useful content and sales copy. A newsletter, should follow the 70/30 rule: It should contain at least 70 percent content (articles, tips, how-to advice, and so forth) and no more than 30 percent sales copy.

6. Include an irresistible special offer, discount, or promotion. These give readers a reason to open your messages and make a purchase.

7. Keep it simple. Computer users have short attention spans. All campaigns should be easy to scan and read.

8. Engage readers. Ask readers to submit feedback, respond to a survey question, or enter a contest.

9. Make sure you are compliant with the CAN-SPAM act by including a link to unsubscribe with every email you send. Visit the FTC Website (*www.ftc.gov/bcp/conline/pubs/ buspubs/canspam.shtm*) for the latest compliance laws.

10. Include all of your contact information, including a physical address, Website, and phone number.

11. Invite subscribers to forward to a friend.

12. Minimize the use of photos and images. Not everyone has high-speed Internet access, and images can make a newsletter difficult to download or may be blocked by the recipients' mail systems.

13. Have your campaign edited for grammar and punctuation. One or two typos are forgivable, but too many and you could hurt your credibility.

14. Use high-contrast colors that are easy to read. Dark letters on light backgrounds (black or blue on white) are the easiest to read and also comply with the Americans with Disabilities Act.

15. Respect your mailing list. Don't send too many messages, or you will risk exhausting your list and will end up with an avalanche of unsubscribe requests.

16. Give readers a reason to look forward to your campaigns. Think about it carefully. Why do they want to read it? How can you make it better? What e-mail campaigns do you love receiving and why? These answers will help you develop a phenomenal publication.

Resources

Popular e-newsletter programs include *www.ConstantContact.com, www.iContact.com,* and *www.Infusionsoft.com.*

75 Sell on eBay

Several years ago, I met an owner of an auto stereo business with multiple store locations, each with a beautiful showroom showcasing a wide variety of high-end stereo systems. It turns out that he had a "ton of overstock" taking up space in the back of his shops. When I asked what he planned to do with it, he shrugged, "I don't know." Say what?

This is a great example of an opportunity for a business to leverage eBay. In the case of the stereo company, the stock was not only wasting space, but it represented a significant amount of cash flow. Even if he sold the equipment off for pennies on the dollar, it would provide a cash boost and solve the problem of ever-growing overstock.

There are all kinds of reasons to consider eBay as a sales channel. One reason is that you can unload overstock either one at a time or in large quantities. You can also sell your regular merchandise and reach a wide variety of potential buyers. Because you can share information about your company in your profile, you have the opportunity to attract buyers directly to your Website—buyers from around the globe.

Small business owners aren't the only ones cashing in on eBay. Some big retailers are liquidating overstock and reaching new customers. Sears, Hewlett Packard, and Dell are just a sample of the retail giants with a presence on eBay.

How It Works

eBay began as a forum for buying and selling collectible items and has morphed into a mammoth online marketplace where millions of items are listed for sale each day. There are dozens of merchandise categories ranging from books, household goods, and antiques to jewelry, concert tickets, computers, airplane parts, and cars.

The community is built on trust as demonstrated through a feedback rating system. After each completed transaction, the buyer can post a rating for the seller of positive, neutral, or negative, along with a brief comment about the quality of the overall transaction. Conversely, the seller can post the same type of rating for the buyer. The goal of any reputable seller is to achieve the highest percentage of positive feedback ratings. Poor feedback ratings or complaints can adversely affect a buyer's decision to purchase from a seller or even get the seller banned from eBay completely.

There are four main formats for selling on eBay:

1. **Traditional Auction:** The seller sets a beginning bid price with a duration of one to 10 days for auction activity. Potential buyers can bid on an item up until the final seconds of the close of auction. The highest bidder wins the auction and is required to send payment to complete the transaction.

2. **Buy It Now:** This is a fixed price format where buyers can avoid bidding via auction and choose to purchase an item immediately.

3. **Dutch Auction:** A seller can list multiple identical items and sell them individually to the highest bidders.

4. **eBay Stores:** This option allows a seller to set up an online store and maintain an inventory of products for sale. Store items can be sold via auction or Buy It Now. This system is ideal for businesses that want to maintain an ongoing inventory and presence on eBay.

Fees and Transactions

You will be charged transaction fees for items sold on eBay, and shipping fees are typically paid by the buyer. As a seller, you can require that buyers send you payments via check or money order, although this can slow the sales process and limit your market reach. Most sellers utilize payment-collection services through a merchant card processor or Paypal. Paypal is a subsidiary of eBay and allows consumers to securely send and receive payments via an e-mail account. There is no fee to sign up as a

Paypal user; however, a small transaction fee is deducted from each payment collected, similar to the fee charged by other merchant card processors.

Give It a Try

Get started by buying some items from other sellers. This is the easiest way to gain an understanding of how the system works. Try both the bidding process and the Buy It Now function to achieve the full buyer experience. This also gives you a chance to establish feedback ratings on your account.

Once you are comfortable as a buyer, start by listing just a few items for sale. Check to see what your competitors are doing. You will want to compete on price and value so be sure you know what you're up against. Soon you could uncover a whole new revenue stream for your business.

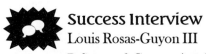

Success Interview
Louis Rosas-Guyon III
R-Squared Computing, Inc.
www.r2computing.com

Year Founded:	1990
Business Partners:	2
Number of Employees:	2 (with about 45 outsourcing partners)

What does your company do?

Business technology coaching and consulting.

Was there a specific turning point when you realized your business was moving to the next level?

It happened in Year 3 of our business. We sold a mid-sized company a single point-of-sale system (computerized cash register) for one of their retail locations. They were very impressed with our professionalism and how quickly we were able to fulfill all their requirements. Within three months we were running the entire company's information technology operations. Our small operation that had hitherto been dealing with small professional services offices suddenly leapt to the next level. We started outsourcing work to local IT providers to manage the client's international operations while we handled the corporate IT strategy to support and improve operations.

What processes or procedures have you implemented that have helped grow your company?

There are a few that immediately spring to mind:

1. **No Jargon:** If we cannot explain the benefits of a technology in simple, plain English then it can serve no business benefit.

2. **Detailed Billing:** All our clients receive detailed billing summaries of all work performed and billed in 15-minute intervals.

3. **Customer Database:** We maintain complete customer records online including work reports, known issues, customer concerns, and so forth. We require outsourced personnel to maintain detailed records using the online system or they don't get paid.

4. **Business First:** All personnel associated with R-Squared are aware that we put our clients first at all times. That means the needs of the customer always supersede ours. So, if you need to work at night or on weekends, that's what we do.

5. **Business Before Tech:** All technology is disruptive. It takes time for anyone to adapt to a new system and/or software. Therefore, all change must be deliberate and managed to ensure minimal disruption of business.

What are some of the best marketing strategies you have used to grow your company?

To date we have invested in the following marketing strategies:

1. **Networking:** I am constantly attending networking events and handing out business cards to anyone and everyone. Sure, I get lots of junk mail, but it also lands me customers.

2. **Word-of-Mouth:** Our customers are our largest source of new clientele. Because I work hard to convert my customers into fanatics, they are always happy to spread the word and introduce me around. I have one customer that invites me to eat lunch with him every two weeks just so he can introduce me to his friends.

3. **Yellow Pages Ad:** By far this was the worst waste of money ever. We cancelled our full-page ad after the first year and have never renewed it. Never again!

4. **Website:** I know everyone is tired of hearing about it, but a Website is mandatory these days. Having a Website may not bring you even one client, but not having a Website will certainly drive them away. A website is all about business credibility. It tells your customers that you are serious enough about your business to spend a few dollars on a Website.

What challenges have you faced and how have you overcome them?

The first challenge we faced was overspending on marketing. We overcame that challenge by shifting to a more personal touch and directly marketing to our friends, neighbors and even our doctors! This simple strategy accounted for all our growth in the first three years.

In Year 2, I accidentally destroyed a customer's laptop. Even though it hurt me financially, I took him to buy a replacement unit the very same day. I then recovered all of his data and transferred it to the new computer free of charge. Because I handled the situation honestly, and I made good on my mistake, I have kept this customer to this day. He has also been the source of the majority of my referrals.

By Year 4 we started running into a series of problems that we nicknamed our "growing pains." It was during this time that we had more work than could possibly be handled by two people in a 24-hour day. The obvious solution was to outsource as much as possible. So, we stopped handling our bookkeeping, accounting, tax preparation, and other business functions in house. This allowed us to focus on our core competencies and gave us the opportunity to strive towards converting our customers into fanatics.

We ran into a terrible cash flow crunch in Year 5. Some of our large customers were paying us on 30-day terms, but our vendors insisted on immediate payment. We handled this by opening a line of credit with our bank. Because we had a strong relationship with the branch manager, we actually got fantastic terms.

In Year 6 we found out that one of our hired hands was a kleptomaniac! I actually caught him in possession of a box of pencils with my client's company name! In addition to pencils, I later found out he had stolen other office supplies, computer equipment, and some personal items people left on their desks. I dealt with this immediately. First, I called the police and filed a complaint. Then I personally called all of the business owners he had access to and informed them of my findings. I asked them to put together a list of missing items from their offices. I then reimbursed all my client's losses for items he could have stolen. I'm sure some of my clients took advantage of me and overcharged me, but it was well worth it. I kept my reputation clear and proved to my customers that I am prepared to make good on mistakes.

The current economic crisis has hit us hard. Roughly 35 percent of my business came from real estate and construction companies. Since those are the industries hardest hit, I have lost many valuable customers. However, we are facing this challenge head on by shifting the sales focus away from these troubled industries. We are actively seeking out largely "recession-proof" industries that dovetail well with our competitive advantage. For example, because we are experts at logistics and shipping systems, we are targeting food distributors as a new client base.

If you were starting over today, what would you do differently?

I wouldn't spend so much money on traditional marketing channels. We spent 80 percent of our startup capital on a year's worth of radio and print advertising. Sadly, this generated no significant business. We almost closed the business after the first year's anemic results. I can admit that I have never been so disheartened. It took Seth Godin's book *Permission Marketing* to get me to finally understand why traditional marketing was no longer viable.

What advice do you have for other business owners?

You asked for it; therefore, in no particular order of importance:

1. DO IT! Stop complaining about your job. Stop talking about your great idea. Roll up your sleeves and get started. Chances are your business idea is not original and there is someone else out there right now working on it, too. If you don't beat them to market then you will have a tougher hill to climb.

2. Don't be afraid to try something new. As a business owner I have been in a situation where I had to tackle a problem even though I had no idea what I was doing! I remember

sitting and arguing with an auditor for the State of Florida's Department of Revenue because they claimed we owned $8,000 in sales tax. We didn't have the money to hire an accountant, so I screwed my courage to the sticking place and fought tooth and nail with the auditor. We settled the account for $250 because I refused to be beaten. The point is you need to be fearless. Sometimes there is no one else there to get the job done.

3. Get to know your bankers! Open a bank account with a local bank and then get to know the bank officers. Try to get on a first-name basis with as many people as possible. This will make it immensely easier later on if you need to get a business line of credit or other types of bank assistance. Because you have a personal relationship with these people, you are far more than just your computer records and account balance history.

4. Reputation is everything. You must have a good reputation or you are dead in the water. All business is personal! Remember: People buy from you, not your company. If you have a sullied reputation, then you will have a tougher mountain to climb. You can control your reputation by being honorable, honest, and forthright. You should also manage your online reputation by being smart about what you post online. Be smart and cautious and you'll be fine.

5. Existing customers are better than prospects. Your existing customers are an amazing source for additional sales. They already know you and trust you. Make sure to offer them new products/services first and at a discount. This will give you a good base to test new products/services with a group that will share their opinions with you.

CHAPTER 11

*"What great thing would you attempt if you knew
you could not fail?"*

—Robert H. Schuller

Social Media Power

76 Climb Aboard the Social Networking Train

Social networking has become a powerful force in business. Sites like Facebook, LinkedIn, and Plaxo provide online business networking opportunities and a chance to build an audience for your business from places far and wide.

You can create a free profile on any of the social networking platforms. I will use Facebook as an example because it is my current favorite. Your profile should include your photo, a description of what you do, links to your Website and blog, work history, educational background, and even a list of personal interests.

After creating a profile, you can search for people you know and send them a "Friend Request." Once your request is accepted, you can view your friend's profile, exchange messages, and view each other's updates.

At the top of your Facebook homepage is a place to update your status. Those who use Facebook for fun might write something like "Jennifer is taking the kids to the movies." When using social networking for business, your status updates should more often relate to what you do: "Looking forward to attending the Technology Expo in Las Vegas tomorrow."

When you post a message to your status, those in your network can view your updates. If you are connected to prospects and customers, some might post a reply to your status such as "I'll be there, too! Let's meet for lunch." The point is to build exposure and find ways to connect and engage your business audience.

You can also post notes to your profile, which provide more space than status updates. You might post a note with a special announcement about a sale that you are running or you could periodically add interesting industry tips. You can also link your notes section to the RSS feed for your blog so that, each time you post a new blog entry, it is added to your profile.

Facebook and many of the other social networking sites also provide applications that you can add to your profile. For example, you can use a blogging application that also features your blog and other people's blogs that you choose as favorites.

If you want to create a profile for your company or a specific product or service that you offer, Facebook guidelines require that you create a "Fan Page." (Only humans are allowed to have an actual profile on Facebook, so you are prohibited from creating your profile as a business name.) A fan page allows you to provide details about your business or the item you want to feature and others can choose to be a fan of your page. This also gives them access to see updates to your page when you make them.

The One With the Most Friends Wins!

While you should start building your friend list by connecting with friends, peers, family, and other people you know, the business opportunity comes from expanding your network outside of your inner circle. To do this, you can start by viewing your friends' list of contacts to see if there are others whom you know but are not yet connected to. Next, you can begin to send requests to those you don't yet know, but would like to know. For example, if you come across a profile for someone in your industry, you could send a friend request with a quick note that says, "Hi, Bill. We are both in the automotive industry. I would love to connect with you and learn more about what you do." When Bill accepts your request, you will have the opportunity to view his updates while he can view yours.

One of the quickest ways to build a substantial list of friends is to join groups. You can search Facebook for any number of topics and find special interest groups where your target audience looms. Join the group and participate in the forums to gain exposure. You can take the initiative to send friend requests to fellow members or sit back and let them reach out to you. Trust me: They will.

A Word of Caution

Sites like Facebook and LinkedIn can be time consuming and addicting. (Facebook is developing a reputation as "Crackbook" because once you start, it's hard to stop!) Manage your time wisely and start with just a couple of sites.

Also, don't discount the fun factor. Thanks to Facebook, I have reconnected with old friends from as far back as grade school. I have heard from past coworkers, third cousins I had lost touch with, and people who I might have otherwise never heard from again. Not only is it fun to reconnect with the past, but I have uncovered business opportunities as a result. We knew each other once in our lives; it makes perfect sense that we could do business together at this stage in our lives.

Resource

Ping.fm—If you manage multiple social networking profiles, this service allows you to post one update that is pushed out to each of your profiles.

77 Gain Visibility With Social Networking Groups

I have recently begun to study how groups work for business and conducted an experiment of my own. I launched a group on Facebook called Entrepreneur-Authors, targeted at business owners who are also authors or aspiring authors. As an author myself and owner of a publishing company with a focus on non-fiction books, this seemed like an ideal niche to carve out.

I was amazed by how the group grew to more than 200 members in less than two weeks with next to no effort on my part. Most interesting was that I generated several solid client leads in the first few days of launching the group and it has become a steady source of leads ever since.

Hosting a group is a passive way of marketing my company. There is no hard sell needed, because members are naturally curious about who is behind the group. It is my job to keep the group interesting and the members engaged. The rest is just gravy.

In researching groups, I found other interesting niches carved out. For example, there are many groups for car enthusiasts. A specialty auto parts company runs a group for Honda owners. How many parts do you think they are selling as a result of this effort?

Groups on LinkedIn.com are also very active and business-oriented. You can post comments in group forums with a link back to your site or start your own group here.

Take advantage of this completely free opportunity to build your own community or participate in communities that are already formed. This is a seriously fun way to make a profit, believe me.

Resource

> *Ning.com*—This innovative platform allows you to create your own social networking platform or join other industry-specific platforms. You will find everything here from networks devoted to specific dog breeds to social networking sites for medical professionals and everything in between.

78 Tweet

Though Twitter falls under the social networking umbrella, it is in a category all its own. Unlike the other social networking sites where you send a friend request and wait for the other person to accept, on Twitter you can choose to "follow" just about anyone.

Members of Twitter post "tweets," which are short status updates, for their followers to view on their profile pages. Twitter is a revolutionary way to get information out quickly while you build a following. For example, when fires were threatening homes in southern California in 2008, firefighters posted status updates on Twitter.

You can follow a wide variety of news sources, celebrities, experts, business owners, authors, and average Joes on Twitter. For example, you might follow CNN to stay on top of news alerts. Talk show hosts like Oprah and Ellen Degeneres post updates about their shows and guests.

For business purposes, the point of Twitter is to share useful information. A chef could post links to recipes while a research firm could post links to case studies. If followers find your tweets interesting, they can re-tweet your post by sending it out to their followers—who may in turn decide to follow you. Devoted Twitter users also search posts for keywords to find industry information. For example, you could search for "coffee" to uncover interesting information and people in the coffee industry (along with those individuals who just like coffee).

The best way to get acquainted with Twitter is to start by setting up a free profile and following others. You can search by keywords to locate people and businesses. Pay attention to posts you find useful and why. This will help you form your strategy and decide whether or not this is right for you.

Twitter is not the right platform for every business, but don't discount it too quickly. I don't believe we've begun to uncover the power of this platform. I personally look forward to seeing how it evolves—and how it affects business growth—in the coming months and years.

79 Harness the Power of a Blog

A blog is essentially an online diary that allows you to post information, tips, thoughts, and ideas in a running log format for others to view. Blogs are used by companies large and small to build an audience, promote business, and gain valuable online exposure.

The major search engines provide higher rankings to sites that update data frequently. When you post to a blog several times each week, you content is constantly changing and growing. The search engines will reward your effort with improved search engine rankings.

One of the top benefits I have found from hosting my blog (Small Business Growth Strategies; *businessinfoguide.com/blog*) is media exposure. Reporters and producers use Google to find sources for stories and, because blogs tend to rank higher with the search engines, there is a good chance that you can land media coverage. After writing several blog posts about "rejecting the recession," I received numerous media calls including interviews for *MORE* magazine and Australia's version of the *Today Show, Sunrise 7.*

A good blog can also attract new customers. People who like what you have to say will pay attention to your blog by subscribing to your blog feed. Hosting a blog is also one of the quickest and easiest ways to showcase your expertise in your subject matter. When you share valuable tips and resources, you engage readers while building credibility in your industry.

It doesn't take long to build up a substantial amount of blog content. You can even repurpose your posts into articles, e-books, books and reports. Many bloggers have found publishing success by building a loyal following online and then impressing publishers with a ready-made online "platform."

Here are some steps to follow when launching a blog that gets noticed:

1. Search the Internet for blogs in your industry and do a little research before you start. Studying other people's blogs will help you identify what you like and don't like, and how you want yours to look and feel.

2. If you already have a Website, check with your hosting provider to see if it provides a blog plug-in option. If not, popular blog services include *www.Typepad.com, www.Wordpress.com,* and *www.Blogger.com.*

3. Establish several categories that appeal to your target audience. For example, my business growth blog has more than a dozen categories, including articles, book recommendations, technology tips, resources for authors, and online marketing. Categories make it easy for readers to browse through past entries.

4. Develop content ideas for your industry. Your blog can include personal opinions, book reviews, links to helpful resources, industry statistics, product recommendations, excerpts from books or white papers (for which you own the copyright), and much more.

5. Keep it simple. Blog entries do not need to be long-winded. In fact, online readers prefer brief content that is easy to scan. I recommend writing just one to three paragraphs for each post. Use sub-headings and bullets to make the text easier to read. Photos and videos can also add visual appeal.

6. Add outgoing links to your blog posts when appropriate. For example, if you mention an article you read in XYZ magazine, make sure to include a hyperlink to the article. Not only will your readers appreciate the option to view the sites you reference, but having links pointing to other sites can further improve your search engine rankings.

7. Schedule time to work on your blog. You should be posting at least three times each week for best search engine optimization. Instead of logging in several times each week, write several blog entries at once and then schedule them to publish on specific days.

8. Promote your blog by including your blog link in your e-mail signature, on your Website, in social networking profiles, and anywhere else you can find to share it with the world. You can also submit it to directories such as *www.BlogCatalog.com* and *www.Technorati.com.*

9. Consider minimizing some of the effort involved by inviting others to contribute. Your blog could include posts by employees, customers, peers, or strategic partners.

10. Maintain your momentum. Be on the lookout for fresh topic ideas so you can avoid getting "blogger's block." When you come across something interesting, get in the habit of writing it down so you have it handy when it's time to update your blog.

80 Gain Blogger Influence

In the age of new media, leveraging other people's blogs is another powerful tool for promotion. Bloggers have tremendous influence. When they recommend a product, their readers buy. Whether a blog is read by a small number of people or tens of thousands, there is a captive audience waiting for suggestions.

These tips will help you get blogger attention:

1. To locate blogs that reach your target audience, try searching keywords at *www.technorati.com,* which ranks the popularity of blogs.

2. Post thoughtful comments on blogs. Someone is paying attention to comments, whether it's the blog owner or the audience, so your comments can get attention. Always include your Website link with your signature. Maybe you'll get lucky and the blogger will contact you or link back to your site.

3. Contact a blogger directly. It can't hurt; the worst that can happen is you won't hear back from him/her. Be brief and to the point. It can help to throw in a genuine compliment that shows you've read what the blogger has to say. For example, "Dear Joe, your post about the discomforts of airline travel was both engaging and right-on. My company manufactures inflatable travel pillows for frequent travelers. Would you consider writing a review if I send you a free sample?"

4. Locate an address and mail a package (product sample, letter, something innovative) to the blog host directly. You never know.

5. Post a complimentary entry in your own blog about the blog you want to reach. Most online marketers track who links to them. Your effort could result in a link back from the site as a thanks or even an inquiry directly from the blogger.

Stacey Kannenberg, author of *Let's Get Ready for Kindergarten!* and *Let's Get Ready for First Grade!,* has benefited from the power of blogs: "My books have been reviewed by over 700 mom blogs and [they] have helped garner my number-one position in the search engines." In fact, several of the entrepreneurs I interviewed cited mentions in other people's blogs as a powerful boost for business.

Getting the attention of bloggers is not an easy task. Popular bloggers are inundated with requests for product reviews and some have strict policies against them.

Aim for quantity. If you can't reach the top-ranked blogs, find blogs that reach a smaller audience. They will likely be easier to get through to. Even a small audience is still going to be a loyal audience, and it all adds up.

81 Host Online Events

Teleseminars, webinars, and virtual conferences can be an exciting and low-cost way to generate big awareness for your business. Seasoned Internet marketers have been using these strategies for years, and, thanks to the affordability and wide reach of online events, more and more companies are using them to expand their reach.

At the 2009 fashion week event in New York, several designers chose to forego the expense of schlepping their wares to an elaborate runway show and instead unveiled their new clothing lines through Webcasts. As a result, designers like Marc Bouwer and R&R were able to show their lines to an international audience—much bigger than the range of people than they would have reached from an event locale in Manhattan.

Companies like Microsoft and Office Depot host free informational teleseminars. This can be a great way to uncover a new audience and introduce them to your business. For example, a law firm could host free one-hour teleseminars on various legal topics and promote them to a wide variety of networks. Someone interested in learning about loopholes in business contracts can sign up and ultimately decide to hire the hosting attorney.

Heidi Richards, founder of Women in eCommerce Association International (*www.wecai.org*), regularly hosts telesummit events for association members. These include a series of informational teleseminars, featuring guest interviews with authors and experts, and are scheduled over a series of days. Virtual events allow members to participate from around the globe.

Steps to Launching Virtual Events

➤ Decide on a topic and how you plan to deliver it. Will it be a Q&A with a guest, will someone interview you, or will you be the sole speaker on the event?

➤ Write a compelling title and description of the event.

➤ Schedule the event several weeks out so that you have time for promotion.

➤ Implement a registration process in order to keep track of attendees if possible.

➤ Promote the event through online and offline networks.

Resources

- Conference call services: *www.FreeConference.com, www.UnlimitedConferencing.com, www.InstantConference.com*
- Webinar services: *www.WebEx.com, www.GoToMeeting.com.*
- Event registration: *www.EventBrite.com.* There is no charge to manage free events, and they charge a small transaction fee for paid events.

Event Promotion Venues

- Create an event on Facebook.

- Post on the wall of any social networking groups that you belong to on Facebook, LinkedIn, and so on.

- Announce your event via Twitter, Facebook, and so forth.

- Post to *www.Craigslist.org* for several cities.

- Post to sites such as *www.SelfGrowth.com,* *www.SeminarAnnouncer.com,* and *www.Events.org.*

Also post to any other sites where your target audience is located. This can include newsletters, message boards, classifieds, paid ads, and any place that can bring exposure for your event.

82 Track Online Activity

You can and should keep track of Websites that mention your company. For example, if someone posts a complimentary blog entry about your business, you will want to know about it in order to thank him/her. Conversely, if someone complains about your company online, you will want to know so that you can take action to resolve any problems.

One of the coolest tools available is Google Alerts (*www.google.com/alerts*). Here you can indicate a keyword, key phrase, or a Web link, and Google will send you an e-mail when your term shows up on a Website, blog, group, or video site. This is completely free and incredibly valuable.

I use keywords to track mentions of my business name, my personal name, titles of my books, and titles of my articles. I also set up alerts for certain key phrases for industries that I follow so that I can discover interesting data related to my field. These alerts have helped me connect with a lot of fantastic people over the years, and have also helped me uncover the occasional virtual violation (when someone has posted one of my articles without permission). I frequently add and update alerts as new needs arise.

Success Interview
Raymond Roberts
Citizant

www.citizant.com

Year Founded:	1999
Business Partners:	Alba M. Alemán (co-founder and president)
Number of Employees:	125

What does your company do?

Citizant provides government professional technical solutions. With a focus on Enterprise Architecture, Application Development, Program Management, and Gov 2.0, Citizant partners with government organizations to develop forward-thinking solutions that create a better future for all citizens.

Was there a specific turning point when you realized your business was moving to the next level?

The $4M to $5M level, in the pure-play technology services market, is the rational limit to what one or two founders can achieve without a rudimentary management team to assist in maintaining momentum. At this stage, one or two individuals have far too many direct reports and back-office issues like payroll, banking, human resources, and contracts begin to assume more gravitational pull than customer satisfaction. It's very easy to become torn between the need to service the customer and the need to have a healthy company with motivated employees.

At this point my business partner and I quickly concluded that we needed to draft the organizational chart for a $10M company and begin the slow, painful process of filling each position with someone other than ourselves. Our first stab at a corporate hierarchy, with departments and reporting structures was not altogether incorrect and many of the basic constructs exist today at twice that size.

It wasn't long before we broke through the barrier of introducing a management team. Many of the people we hired back then to fill those rolls stayed with our company for a long time. They were instrumental in helping the company to get on the track of year-over-year growth.

We discovered the same hurdle around the $10M revenue mark. This time, it was the middle layer of management that needed to be introduced and formalized. Again, new hires were made and many of those people played pivotal roles in moving the company forward, inch by inch.

We never hit home runs; we never got a hole in one. Our business growth has been a game of inches. We played hard every day, and with sheer effort, discipline, and tenacity, we added up the inches and came up with a new revenue achievement every quarter, and every year.

I think the next level for us is just around the corner. I say this because we have begun to turn all of our energy on creating value for the marketplace. In doing that, something interesting has happened. Really amazing people with extraordinary talent and capability have begun taking interest in Citizant as a company of choice. People are referring colleagues that they respect, senior managers are beginning to reconstitute high-performing teams from previous employers, and thought leaders from within the industry are beginning to call us to discuss their future. That has got to be a turning point!

What processes or procedures have you implemented that have helped grow your company?

We did some things in perhaps a counter-intuitive manner. For some reason, we focused as much management attention on the business as on the customer. We were fascinated by the idea that internal processes needed to be strong and that there was an order and a discipline to the central nervous system of a business. We approached the customer from the inside out—meaning, we believed that our customers would be satisfied not only by the top-notch technologists that we hired to solve their problems, but by the fact that we had a well run company to support them. Too often we heard from the marketplace about fast rising competitors who fell on their own swords of too little infrastructure. We surmised that great customer services meant more that great front-line people. There had to be something more substantial in the back office to support them with their customers.

So we went ahead and built out very robust procedures and processes to manage our finance, human resources, contracts, and recruiting. Our goal was to build in quality, repeatability, safety, and speed. Not all of those variables work together; speed seems to be sacrificed every time. The trick is to right-size processes and that is difficult to do in a company that is constantly changing size and dimension every quarter.

Two important strategic processes that we have adopted are disciplined planning and, more recently, business development.

Our planning processes have grown from some sophomoric hand-drawn concepts to much more robust and formal modeling. We involve a broad audience over several months and think deeply about our business. We never make radical changes—but rather tweak our model to gain velocity and momentum. The frustrating thing about planning is that it's just not done often enough, and the team can never get great at it fast enough. Annual planning is too important to mess up, yet we have expected ourselves and our managers to shift from daily tactical thinking to long-term strategic thinking for a brief period each year with the hope that somehow we could emerge from a three-day session with a great plan. The truth is that planning is something you get good at after several years. It's probably something we should have received more coaching on.

Most recently, business development has taken on a new meaning. We have truly started to formalize elements of this art, and we have created some collaborative rules and disciplines that help a team of very smart, technically inspired people do something that is not easy or natural for them to do. We chase a few large deals and that requires some rather sophisticated processes and leadership. We are beginning to create a mind-shift in our company around the notion of creating new revenue streams from new assignments. We have implemented a "seller-doer" model and, without the aid of "sales" people, we have enabled our people to pursue large deals, which they have a strong desire to deliver on should they land the deal. This has proven to be the most difficult and complex set of processes and procedures because selling is often more art than science.

Of course some procedures and processes can be external recognized. Citizant is an ISO 9001:2000 certified company and we expect to be appraised at Maturity Level 3 by the Carnegie Melon Software Engineering Institute's Capability Maturity Model by the time this book is in print.

What are some of the best marketing strategies you have used to grow your company?

Citizant is a professional technical services company. We help our customers solve complex business problems with information technology solutions.

One of the best methods that we employ is the positioning of subject matter experts in front of prospective customers. By attracting people with some "star" status within specific technology niches (like information security or enterprise architecture), we draw attention to our company as a credible and capable vendor. Customers pay attention to this, and often accept meetings and invitations based on the fact that a subject matter specialist will be available to discuss customer challenges.

While the sales process in our market space is far more involved than this one element, and an entire team of people is required to close a deal, this approach of using "stars" has proven quite effective.

What challenges have you faced and how have you overcome them?

Again—it's about people. Nothing in business happens without people. Aligning company goals with the skills, personalities and motivations of a large group of people is a very challenging activity. Making career decisions that affect good people is quite stressful. The art of finding and hiring the right person for the right job at the right time in a company's maturity and life cycle is not so easy.

If you were starting over today, what would you do differently?

A dozen years of working a market teaches you a few things. My next venture will still be boot-strapped by founder/operators, but with a broader portfolio of investors than simply founder/operators.

The management team will be significantly more senior, even at the beginning, and all of them will have a stake in the outcome from outset. People, especially those in positions of high impact, need to have a long-term commitment to the outcome of the company. In theory, this can help people stay more objective about their position at the company and focus less on personal drama.

What advice do you have for other business owners?

Focus on your business and spend a great deal of energy on your customers and employees. Keep your ego out of it. Do not let yourself be the center of attention—that's your customer's role. Do not assume that because you have issued a directive that somehow it will get done by your people without your clear and involved leadership and participation. Do not confuse an order or a command as an easy way around the hard work that leadership actually demands.

Everyone at your company needs daily coaching and leadership. The very best professional athletes do not win games on their own. Do not assume that you can abdicate your role as a coach and leader. You must be prepared to role up your sleeves and work side by side with your people to motivate, inspire, and coach them to succeed. Otherwise, you will be disappointed by the results.

Business ownership is something that you must learn to leave in the parking lot before you enter the office every morning. In the office, you are a leader and a coach. It is very difficult to separate yourself from the fact that you are the owner of your business while acting as its operator. There is no doubt that the level of personal and financial risk that you bear as an owner eclipses any other risk that your employees might bear in business. HOWEVER, nobody cares, and nor should they. And most of our feelings about ownership have more to do about our egos than reality. You've worked hard to get to where you are. You have taken enormous risks to get here. You should be entitled to be more in charge, more in command, and less overworked, but the truth is, if you want to continue growing, your work has just begun. It never ends. You must focus on your customers and your people and leave your personal fears, anxieties, feelings, and your ego at the door every day.

Running a business is only glamorous if that's what you want out of it. If you want a pay-day, then you need to build value—and that takes hard work, perseverance, and an ability to inspire people. None of this involves ego.

Part Four

Prosper
(Maintain the Momentum)

CHAPTER 12

"Luck is what happens when preparation meets opportunity."

—Lucius Annaeus Seneca, philosopher

Big Business Decisions

83 Get the Right Corporate Structure

I see so many businesses running as sole proprietorships, something that I also did for many years. However, once I finally understood the importance of protecting my assets, not to mention the tax advantages of choosing the right entity, I made some important changes.

Garrett Sutton, an attorney and author of numerous books, including several of the *Rich Dad, Poor Dad* series with Robert Kiyosaki, says that asset protection is one of the most important reasons to incorporate: "A corporation protects your home and bank accounts from claims against your business. As a sole proprietor, if you get sued, everything you've worked for your entire life can be put at risk."

Sutton stresses the importance of choosing the right entity early on. "Even if you run as a sole proprietor for a month and then decide to incorporate, if someone files a lawsuit based on something that occurred during that first month, your assets are still going to be vulnerable." Another little-known benefit of incorporating is that you are less likely to become the target of an IRS audit, because they are far more interested in pursuing sole proprietors.

Because a lawsuit can be detrimental to your business, it may make sense to form multiple entities. For example, if you own rental properties, each can be set up in an individual LLC. Then, if a renter in one of your properties files a lawsuit, your other properties will be insulated from any judgment that is awarded. Along the same lines, Sutton advises, "You should consider forming a separate entity for your trademarks and other intellectual property so that they are protected in the event of a lawsuit."

Choosing the right entity for your business depends on what you want to accomplish. "An LLC may offer better flow-through taxation benefits and asset protection; however, an S-Corp can help minimize payroll taxation," says Sutton. "There is no right or wrong answer, which is why it's important to talk to an advisor."

For additional information, talk to a professional advisor such as your accountant or attorney. Resources are also available through Garrett Sutton's site (*www.CorporateDirect.com*).

84 Manage Overhead Expenses

Last year I decided to move out of my home office and into a commercial office space. I found the perfect location, installed new carpet, ordered furniture, decorated it with pictures of my son, and officially moved in. I immediately realized I had made a mistake.

I missed working at home—having my cats at my feet, working in sweats when I felt like it, and knowing that I was in my most comfortable space. My new office felt stale and lonely. It was an expensive lesson. I ended up using the office a couple of times per month for meetings, and let it go when the lease expired.

It's easy to acquire business expenses; the challenge is distinguishing between a worthwhile and necessary expense and one that will leave you with a spending hangover.

I have to share with you the story of Chris, the owner of a multi-million-dollar commercial flooring business. He defies nearly all of the strategies outlined in this book. Chris doesn't have a business plan or a marketing plan. He doesn't obsess about setting goals. He doesn't have a Website or a single employee on the payroll. Yet he grosses several million dollars each year.

I used to joke that Chris was an "accidental entrepreneur," but the truth is that he is successful for several reasons.

1. He doesn't like to spend money, even though he's got plenty to spare. He's never considered renting an office and instead runs his entire business from his Blackberry, which makes his operation portable. He spends about five percent of his time working at his desk, about 20 percent of his time "working" from his vacation home in Lake Tahoe, and the rest of the time he is conducting business in his car, while laying by the pool, or wherever he happens to be on a given day.

2. Chris doesn't have any employees. In the world of commercial flooring (carpet and floors for retail stores, fitness centers, etc.), it is not uncommon to use sub-contractors for installations. He also has an independent bookkeeper, CPA, and attorney.

3. He is the classic middle man. Chris's responsibilities include fielding sales calls, locating and hiring contractors, keeping client relationships going (often from a golf course), and managing cash flow. He doesn't install anything himself or provide any labor.

4. He has several credit lines, but doesn't use them. He pays for everything in cash.

5. He picks and chooses which jobs he oversees. For example, he is always happy to hop on a plane to inspect a job in Maui or Las Vegas. For most other jobs, he delegates that responsibility to a contractor.

6. Aside from flyers he gave out to apartment complexes in his first year of business, he doesn't spend a dime on traditional marketing. Instead, his business is built on relationships and word-of-mouth. His marketing budget is spent on dinners, golf outings, and occasional trips with clients.

7.   He eliminated low-dollar clients in the early years. Chris used to provide services for consumers (carpet, tile, and flooring for private homes), but discovered that he earned far more money on a few large corporate jobs than he did managing many small home jobs. As a result, when the recession hit and consumers stopped indulging in home upgrades, his business was unaffected. Corporate clients still needed to maintain floors.

Lessons Learned

It's entirely possible to be an uber-successful one-person show. Chris's business model is not without fault. He is well aware that he has built a business that he couldn't sell because his relationships are too dependent on him. But right now, he doesn't care. He's got cash in the bank, a steady stream of business, minimal expenses, and a flexible lifestyle. I'm afraid he's an anomaly.

He's also my little brother.

When I asked if I could write about his story, he laughed. "Sure. Why not?" He was on his way up the mountain to spend a long weekend at the lake. When I invested in my commercial office last year, he was the first one to ask why I was wasting money on office space when I had a perfectly nice office at home. He also taunts me about my Starbucks habit and the fact that I get my car washed on a regular basis.

Chris is the quintessential millionaire next door. He cleans his own pool and his 3,000-plus-square-foot house. He washes his Escalade in the driveway and drives across town on Tuesdays for free slice night at his favorite pizza joint. He is selective about how he spends money and as a result, owned two homes before his 30th birthday.

We are faced with opportunities to spend our money every day. I will admit to erring on the side of spending. I'm not afraid to invest in something that promises to improve my business or life in some way. But when it comes to business growth, we have a responsibility to use discretion before opening the checkbook. Do you really need that office? Maybe you do! But maybe you don't. Weigh your options carefully.

85 Rent Commercial Space

Following my remorseful experience in renting an office I rarely used, the reality is that many businesses will face a time when commercial space becomes a necessity. I also owned a retail store, and negotiating the lease was a surprisingly vulnerable experience. Following is the advice I wish I'd had when I did this for the first time.

Renting a commercial space is a lot different than renting the apartment you had in college. Commercial real estate is an industry all its own, and you would be well advised to have someone on your side. A real estate broker who specializes in commercial property can not only help you locate the right space, she can help you navigate and negotiate a long, baffling list of terms and conditions.

Commercial leases should be reviewed with great care. The best option is to have a lawyer review it. At the very least, your broker can assist you in understanding what is typical and where you have some wiggle room. Make sure you read the fine print; there can be all kinds of "gotchas" hidden in commercial leases.

For example, some contracts stipulate that the renter is responsible for maintaining the heating and air conditioning systems. Repairs to a commercial HVAC system can be quite expensive, so consider this when comparing locations.

You shouldn't have to accept a lease at face value. In most cases, the landlord expects to make revisions. Ask questions about the terms you don't understand and decide what is most important to you.

Avoid over-committing to the length of the agreement. If your business plan is only for three years and you think you might want to sell or expand after that time, then don't sign a five-year lease. (They will always attempt to lock you in for the longest possible period.)

The landlord is going to try to get the best deal from you, so it's up to you to negotiate a better deal. If improvements need to be made to the building and the landlord leaves you with this task, then it is perfectly reasonable to request free rent in return. In fact, most landlords expect to offer at least one or two months of free rent to allow you time to make improvements.

You may have more bargaining power if the space has been empty for a while and you know the landlord is eager to rent it. In this case, ask for additional months at half the normal rental fee. The landlord is a business owner, too, and worries about cash flow just as you do. If you offer to pay six months at half rent, you will essentially receive three months of free rent. This is a perfectly reasonable request if the space needs a fair amount of work or has been vacant for a while. It also creates a win-win situation, because the landlord is still collecting some amount of rent each month while giving you an opportunity to get your new space up and running.

The bottom line is that it is up to you to ask for what you need. You may have to push your broker to ask tough questions. When I negotiated my first space, my broker—who had been in business for 30+ years—insisted that I was asking for too many changes to the lease. But guess what? Most of my requests were granted or at least met halfway. You won't know unless you ask.

86 Buy the Building

Depending on your financial situation, you may want to consider buying the building where your business will be located. One option is to buy a multi-unit building with existing tenants who pay enough rent to cover a good majority of the mortgage, while leaving you enough space to operate your business.

The Small Business Administration has a special loan program for fixed assets such as commercial land or a building. The CDC/504 program typically includes a lien from a bank for up to 50 percent of the cost, up to 40 percent backed by the SBA with the help of a Certified Development Company (CDC), and at least 10 percent funded by the buyer. For additional information, visit *www.SBA.gov* or discuss this opportunity with your banker.

Also, be sure to discuss the tax implications with your accountant and insurance requirements with your insurance broker. Your attorney should be consulted as well. Owning the building may sound like a grand opportunity, but know what you're getting yourself into before you get too far along in the process.

87 Protect Your Business Legally

Worrying about potential legal issues can be like anticipating a natural disaster. Nobody wants to think about disastrous situations, but, when one strikes, you want to make sure you are prepared. Having a legal protection plan is like the disaster kit you have stored in your closet. You hope that you never have to use it, but you feel safer because you know it's there.

Marjorie Jobe is a business attorney in El Paso, Texas, and author of *The Business Law Battle Plan for Entrepreneurs: Protect Your Company from Lawyers, Lawsuits and Other Legal Disasters.* I asked her to share her top three legal protection strategies; here's what she had to say:

1. Pay close attention to the contractual provisions in any contract that you sign. You can control how an agreement can be terminated, control the law that applies, control where a

dispute will be resolved, and limit or eliminate the threat of a courtroom battle with an arbitration requirement. In short, contracts allow you to control your legal destiny with regard to the subject of the contract and any disagreements that flow from it.

2. Employee lawsuits are the new minefield for plaintiffs' lawyers who are being shut out of the personal injury area with tort reform. If you have employees, adopt specific employee policies that can protect you from employee lawsuits, and then follow those policies in hiring and firing employees. Of particular importance are policies dealing with the use of the Internet and e-mails by employees. Many businesses have not kept up with the expanding role of the Internet in their daily operations and have no policies or very vague policies on the access to and use of the Internet.

3. Be diligent in keeping good records of your income and expenses and in paying taxes. It is critical that any financial statements and loan or lending applications be accurate and up to date. Making a mistake on your income or asset disclosures to lenders is dangerous and reckless. Additionally, one of the most common reasons that new and small businesses fail is the failure to pay payroll and sales taxes promptly. Be conservative in completing loan applications, capitalize your business properly and pay all taxes before you pay yourself.

Whether you anticipate legal concerns or not, establishing a relationship with a business attorney can give you an advocate when you need one and can ensure that your business is on the right track. "Although an attorney is not necessary for the review of every contract, every business operator should be educated by an experienced attorney on the important provisions of contracts and what to include in or to avoid when entering into any agreement," says Jobe.

If you ever find yourself in any kind of legal trouble, Jobe recommends calling your attorney immediately—before you answer any questions. "Attorneys should handle all inquiries or contacts by any investigatory or law enforcement arm of the federal or any state agency," said Jobe. "Subpoenas of records, calls from investigators, and other inquiries can lead to real criminal repercussions if not handled correctly."

The bottom line is that having an attorney on your team is another form of insurance. Though most of us don't anticipate a legal problem, that doesn't mean that we aren't vulnerable. Getting the right protection before you have a problem is like having good medical insurance before you are hit by a bus. If you wait until after you are incapacitated, you will have lost your leverage.

⚡ 88 Consider Marital Property Agreements

I must admit that, before reading *The Business Law Battle Plan for Entrepreneurs* by Marjorie Jobe, I didn't know anything about marital property agreements or why they are important. As it turns out, the state of your marital bliss is only one of several considerations when it comes to these agreements. Here's what you need to know:

1. **Divorce Proceedings:** According to Jobe, "If you or your business partners (if you have any) encounter divorce proceedings, marital property agreements protect your business and its original members from the reach of spouses."

   For example, if you have a business partner who owns a 50-percent stake in your business and he gets a divorce, his spouse could be awarded a share in your company. Soon you could have two partners who are potentially at war with each other—and end up in a situation that could be detrimental to your company.

2. **Borrowing Power:** Without a marital property agreement, obtaining business financing could hinge on your spouse's

credit. Jobe says, "A marital property agreement can increase the borrowing capability and available capital of the family, especially if both spouses are separate business owners."

For example, if you and your spouse both own businesses and your spouse has outstanding business debt, that can work against you when you seek financing for your company. A marital property agreement allows you to treat your respective companies as separate entities so that the credit status of each spouse is viewed separately when obtaining financing.

3. **Protection From Lawsuits:** Even the most ethical company can become the target of lawsuit or a criminal investigation. If the feds target your company or you find yourself the victim of a lawsuit," Jobe says, "a marital property agreement can protect your family from forfeiture of all family assets in the event of criminal proceedings or liability of the business operator."

For example, if the feds target your business for an investigation, they can seize your assets and even freeze your accounts. (The power that they have is frightening.) If the business is protected under a marital property agreement, your family's assets should be insulated from the process.

The good news is that marital property agreements can be entered into before or after a marriage. Jobe recommends that each spouse retains their own lawyer in reviewing or negotiating the terms of the agreement.

 **Success Interview**
Gary Nealon
RTA Cabinet Store
www.rtacabinetstore.com
Year Founded: 2006
Number of Employees: 6

What does your company do?

Importer of kitchen cabinets and bathroom vanities. We sell to retail stores, contractors/builders, and homeowners.

Was there a specific turning point when you realized your business was moving to the next level?

We started the business with a small showroom and a Website. We were buying from another company and having them ship the product for us. The first year we had some traffic, but the business really wasn't taking off. After doing a lot of research of marketing strategies and Internet marketing, I started implementing my own Internet marketing techniques. The company really started taking off once I was able to get our first site up to the number-one ranking on Google for several of the keyword searches. We now rank in the top five for over 20 different keywords. I also started implementing some free methods of local advertising on the Internet, which now brings in 10–15 clients a week that we never had before.

What processes or procedures have you implemented that have helped grow your company?

Internet marketing was the first step in the process. Once we had a significant amount of traffic, we started looking at ways to increase the average sale. I researched complementary products and add-ons that we could use to up sell our customers. On average, we were able to add an additional $200 per transaction by offering additional products after the initial purchase.

What are some of the best marketing strategies you have used to grow your company?

Internet marketing by far has produced the best results, and is the easiest to track and measure. I have tried mass mailings, newspaper, print, and magazine. Implementing SEO strategies, Google Adword campaigns, and taking advantage of Craig's List ads are the three biggest sources of new business for us.

What challenges have you faced and how have you overcome them?

Believe it or not, rapid growth has been the biggest challenge. Making the transition from a retail showroom to an importing/wholesale business has been a challenge. Finding a building, sourcing product from overseas, and adding staff to take on specific responsibilities has been a challenge.

If you were starting over today, what would you do differently?

Knowing what I know now, I would have focused all of my efforts on Internet marketing from the beginning. Using the strategies that I now know, we could have saved a lot of time and money that we spent on trying to find the right way to market the business.

What advice do you have for other business owners?

No matter how small your business is or how local your target market is, you still need to have a Website and market to those customers. Recent studies have shown that more people now search for local businesses on the search engines than they do by using the phone book. Most Internet marketing techniques are free, and you can literally dominate the competition by running local ads and optimizing your Website to target local customers.

CHAPTER 13

"The future belongs to those who prepare for it today."

—Malcolm X

Keep an Eye on the Future

89 Improve Personal Productivity

One of the greatest lessons I have learned about productivity is how to organize tasks. I have always kept a to-do list, yet I still felt overwhelmed. Then I learned that each project on the list needs to include a list of sub-tasks. These are the action items that need to be achieved in order to complete a project.

David Allen, author of *Getting Things Done: The Art of Stress Free Productivity,* says, "Listing three goals you want to achieve for the year is different than the 65 projects you need to complete to get there."

"Most lists are incomplete and create pressure and stress," says Allen. "Are you making decisions about the outcomes you're committed to and the actions you want to take?" Allen also recommends delegating tasks: "Define who needs to take the project and assign it."

For example, if you are preparing a presentation for a potential new client, the primary project is "Client Presentation." The sub-tasks or action items might include:

- Research the company.
- Compile notes from sales team. (Delegate to Judy.)
- Gather sales brochures.
- Bring a sample.
- Write a proposal.
- Update the PowerPoint presentation.

232 ~ LEAP! 101 Ways to Grow Your Business

By itself, "Client Presentation" is not an action item. It's the sub-tasks that will keep you up at night, hoping you don't forget something. Writing tasks down with actions has by far been one of my best moves toward productivity.

Sometimes my task list can get pretty long. In order to stay on top of deadlines, I prioritize what needs to be accomplished first. I also schedule blocks of time in my calendar to work on projects. I treat projects like any other appointment; otherwise, I won't leave myself enough time to get them done.

There is something rewarding about getting to the end of the week with a task list that is covered with check marks of completion. On Fridays, I copy any remaining tasks on to a fresh list to use on Monday. I review my calendar, schedule time for important projects, and end the week feeling in control.

Also, for goals and tasks I want to tackle in the long run, I keep a running list called "Eventually." As business owners, most of us have no shortage of ideas. When I think of a new marketing strategy or an idea for a product or course, I note it on my Eventually list. I periodically review the list and decide when it's time to move something to my main task list. This is gives me added insurance that my ideas won't disappear into thin air. (If I let them run around in my head, they could get chased off by other ideas!) And it gives me a chance to prioritize them at a later date.

If you're in a productivity slump, give this method a try. Your task list can be electronic or on a sheet of paper. (I use a 6x9 spiral notepad.) List tasks for each goal or project, delegate what you can, and prioritize the rest.

90 Take Control Over E-Mail

If your in box has become your arch enemy, know that you are not alone. I hear a lot of people complaining about being buried under e-mail (myself included), and the truth is, it is only going to get worse unless you do something about it now.

When you receive an e-mail, someone is seeking your attention. It's up to you to decide how or if you are going to respond. David Allen, author of several books, including *Getting Things Done,* says that e-mail essentially equates to someone needing your attention: "E-mail is no different than someone stopping you in the hall."

One way to take back control is to touch everything just once. As e-mail comes in, you can either respond immediately or use folders to get organized. "Most people don't make the distinction between what is meaningful," says Allen. "Once you decide the meaning, you can decide where to park it."

Here are some of the types of folders you can designate:

> Urgent Response Needed.

> Respond This Week.

> To Read. (Use for newsletters, industry publications, etc.)

> Clients (one folder for each).

> Vendors (one folder for each).

> Reference (topics you want to cover in your blog, social networking, etc.).

> Employees and Contractors (one folder for each).

> Groups (messages pertaining to any group you are involved with).

> Smile File (notes of appreciation or anything that brightened your day).

> Testimonials (letters of praise from clients; ask for their permission to reprint!).

> Projects (one folder for each so that you can keep track).

> Social Networking (requests from networks like Facebook, Twitter, LinkedIn, etc.).

> Personal Folders. (You might keep one for photos, messages from your family, etc.)

To get the most out of your folders, set up e-mail filters that pre-screen mail for you. If you use Microsoft Outlook, you can create rules that automatically route e-mail to designated folders. Your social networking requests should get automatically placed in a folder so they don't cause constant interruption in your day. Newsletters and offers from your favorite vendors can go in the "To Read" folder. Then designate time in your schedule each week to go through them.

Allen says it's the volume of e-mail that overwhelms people. "Turn the sucker off and then deal with it." He advises checking e-mail just a couple of times each day, which isn't always easy to do.

Whenever I get overwhelmed with e-mail, I remind myself that the world won't come to an end if I can't get to it as quickly as I would like. If it's urgent, you would hope that person picks up the phone instead.

I also find it amusing that I can spend hours on e-mail in a given day. Then, after being out for a day, I'll expect to spend hours on it when I return. But when I do, it takes just a fraction of the time I anticipate. Allen's advice is sound: once you assign meaning to a message, you can decide what to do with it. The key is to take action immediately. E-mail is a business tool and works best when used for its intended purpose.

91 Develop a Goal Plan

New Year's Eve is my favorite holiday. I love the symbolism of passing from one year to the next, as I always expect that the coming year will be even better than the current year. Year after year, they just keep getting better.

To prepare for the new year, I create a new goal plan and review my goal plans from previous years. A goal plan is a list of goals you intend to achieve for the year. I include a mix of simple goals (like joining a new trade association) and specific goals (like adding x number of new customers to my roster), as well as some that seem slightly beyond my reach (I always stretch my income goals). Year after year I am amazed by how many goals I achieve.

It's interesting in reviewing previous years because some goals may take two or three years to achieve. Some goals fall off the list entirely because I changed direction. It's not a scorecard. It's a tool to help me stay focused.

Last year I added a new step in my goal-planning process. I ended the year by listing all of my accomplishments. I used my calendar to fill in details of things I had done, places I had been, and new alliances forged. Outside of my goals, I was able to celebrate many other achievements that I hadn't planned.

My goals list gets posted above my desk each year so I can review it periodically. It is a road map for where I am going personally and professionally. It is a right of passage that I look forward to completing each year.

Here are some prompts to help you create your goals list:

➤ How much money do I want to earn?

➤ How much time will I spend with my kids?

➤ How much time will I spend with my spouse?

➤ How much time will I give myself?

➤ When does my workday begin and end?

➤ How often will I exercise?

➤ What new skills do I want to learn?

➤ Who will I hire to help me grow my business?

➤ What specific strategies will I add to grow my business?

➤ What events do I plan to attend?

➤ What vacations do I plan to take?

➤ What specific changes will I make in my business?

➤ What specific changes will I make in my personal life?

➤ Who do I want to know or connect with?

➤ How will my business look different a year from now?

➤ What do I need to say no to?

➤ What do I need to say yes to?

➤ What are my top priorities for the coming year?

➤ What processes do I need to put in place to run a better business?

➤ How many books will I read this year?

➤ How will I improve my customers' experience?

➤ What do I need to improve in my life?

92 Hire a Coach

I met Jenifer Landers of FullyExpressedCoaching.com a couple of years ago through the local business community. She's a life coach and I told her, "Wow—I know a lot of screwed-up people who could use your services!"

It wasn't long before we became friends and would periodically meet up for coffee or lunch. One day as I was driving back from an outing with Jenifer, I realized that she always left me thinking about things in a different way. Even in casual conversation she managed to weave in nuggets of wisdom. I called her before I even made it back to my office: "I want to try out this coaching thing. Sign me up!"

Though "life coach" is an emerging title, it's not a new concept. For generations, masters of business have turned to others for mentoring, advice, and coaching on all different levels. As I have since learned from Jenifer, coaching is not for "screwed-up people." Coaching is a tool for successful people who are blocked or struggling with some aspect of life. Many of us are Type-A personalities. We are wound up, full of ideas and passion, yet we are not perfect. Nobody is perfect. I certainly am not perfect.

Unlike traditional therapy, coaching is not about digging up your past to uncover why you behave the way you do. It's about uncovering blocks that are holding you back in some way and finding the answers within yourself to move forward.

To put it into context, I'll share a bit about my journey. In business, I am goal-oriented, driven, and controlling of my surroundings, and have high expectations of myself and those I hire. My expectations on the world around me were zapping a lot of my energy, especially when it came to my marriage.

I have control over most of my workday. I can write down a goal or a task and make it happen. What I had to learn is that when it came to my family life, I couldn't just snap my fingers and turn my husband into the person I wanted him to be at that moment. I was putting unrealistic expectations on him. Jenifer helped me become a better wife. (My husband often jokes about sending her gifts of thanks.)

Hiring a coach, whether to deal with life issues or business issues or a little of both, can be a great outlet for business owners who feel stuck in some way. If your life isn't as rewarding as you would like it to be, a coach can help you find ways to make it better.

Maybe a coach will give you the permission you need to take care of yourself, take a day off, give up a relationship that isn't serving you, or improve a relationship that you cherish. Maybe it's the nudge you need to remove roadblocks that are keeping you from moving to the next level.

93 Play a Bigger Game

Last year I sent a note to my mastermind group that said, "I want to play a bigger game." I was feeling buried under details and things that didn't really matter to me personally or professionally. I was unfocused, overwhelmed, and ready to make some big changes. That statement inspired a series of changes for all of us.

First of all, I went through a list of obligations and un-obligated myself. I was serving on advisory boards long past their value to me. I was in the habit of saying yes to everything without qualifying how it would affect me, and then resenting the time it took away from doing something that mattered. I learned that every time I said yes to something, I had to say no to something else.

Time is our most important commodity. There's never enough of it and, aside from hiring out as much of the work as you can, you can't buy time. Every minute in your day matters, especially with a family at home who deserves all the quality you can bring to your life together.

Now when a new opportunity presents itself, I ask, "Is this helping me play a bigger game?" For example, if I'm asked to speak, I ask a lot more questions than I used to. Who is the audience? What does it pay? How much time will it take away from my life? Does it make sense in my big picture?

Playing a bigger game has improved my focus. It forces me to keep my eye on the ball. Nobody likes to say no, and I am challenged with this daily. But at some point, you have to put yourself back at the top of the priority list. Otherwise you are just going to be swimming against the tides, always fighting and exhausted. At some point you have to declare that enough is enough. You have to have a vision of your future and make sure that "opportunities" align with that vision.

How can you play a bigger game?

94 Give Back

Ask anyone who is tremendously successful what they get from giving back to the world, and they will tell you that the rewards are immense. When we give to charity, whether in money or our time, we get it back in multiple. It's called karma, baby. Do good and the good comes back. Pay it forward.

I love it when I shop at a store that asks if I would like to donate $1 to charity. Whether it's Saint Jude's Children's Hospital, Make-a-Wish Foundation (they accept donations of your unused frequent flyer miles!), Susan G. Koman Breast Cancer Foundation, the Humane Society—they all matter, and it's an opportunity to give. A dollar is so insignificant when it leaves your wallet, yet can have such an impact on the world.

Imagine what would happen if EVERY business supported a charity. What if we ALL had a cause?

- What if instead of selling your used car and dealing with looky-loos and countless phone calls generated from a classified ad, you donated it to an organization that could benefit from it?

- What if instead of wasting a Saturday holding a garage sale, you gave all the items to your local women's shelter?

- What if you made a tradition out of taking your family to the homeless shelter on Thanksgiving to serve, give back, and remember how lucky you are?

If everyone found a way to give, we would cure illnesses, save lives, rescue animals, give people in dire straits a place to turn, and provide food, shelter, education, and medicine to those who didn't have it. We would make the world a better place.

I know I'm an optimist, but I see an opportunity for all of us in the small business community to make a change here. Even a small shift could have a big impact. So the next time you're asked to donate a dollar, increase it to five or 10 or 50. Sponsor a friend on charitable walk. Buy a ticket to a charity event and enjoy a date night with your spouse. Host a charitable event through your business and involve your customers. Seize the opportunity to make a difference. Pay it forward.

Success Interview
Nicole DeBoom
SkirtSports, Inc.
Boulder, Colorado
www.skirtsports.com

Year Founded:	Incorporated September 2004, First sales in February 2005
Business Partners:	I founded the company. My husband, Tim, and I retain the vast majority of the business at this point.
Number of Employees:	8 full-time, 2 part-time

What does your company do?

We manufacture and sell women's fitness apparel (SkirtSports) and produce and operate a national running race series (SkirtChaser 5k Series).

What led you to start your business?

I was a professional triathlete looking for something fun and exciting to wear. Most of the athletic apparel was very masculine and I have always operated under the mantra "look good, feel good, perform better."

I decided to start a company that emphasized femininity within athleticism. It would be okay to look like a woman while beating the men!

Was there a specific turning point when you realized your business was moving to the next level?

There continue to be many turning points. The first was probably when we had to commit our first real chunk of change! It was in November 2004 and we invested $5,000 to buy a large quantity of skirts. It was a true commitment.

Looking back, it's easy to identify the levels. We started as an online business. That was one level. Then stores wanted our product and we needed to determine how the wholesale side of the business would work. That was another level. Then we decided to start our own race series to promote and market our products. That opened the door to an entirely new business model and a new brand for men. The levels never really stop. I think they are determined by either a new financial investment or entry into a new category or business model.

What processes or procedures have you implemented that have helped grow your company?

Sales distribution channels have been key. We started working with independent sales reps and have noticed immediate growth in regions that are supported by our reps. We also hired a full-time ecommerce director. Until a year ago, the online store was our largest revenue generator, and we didn't even have a full-time committed employee working on it. That was an important hire.

Focusing on our strengths is something that has helped us grow the business. This includes product direction first and foremost. Everyone suggests a new path (tennis or golf wear, team sports, lifestyle, etc), but staying true to our focus has been important. It's easy to get off track with so many great opportunities.

What are some of the best marketing strategies you have used to grow your company?

"Convert to Skirt" was our first national marketing campaign in 2007. We asked people to send in their old running shorts and they would get a SkirtSports skirt at a discount. We then recycled or donated the shorts to women in need.

It was very attention-grabbing. We titled our press release "SkirtSports wants your shorts!"

The problem came in the form of channel conflict. We only offered this promotion through our online store. We started receiving phone calls from our retailers that their customers were demanding a discount to match ours (15 percent, which really only paid for shipping). We tried to initiate a program through our stores but couldn't get the leverage going.

Our new strategy came in the form of the 2008 SkirtChaser national 5k race series. Again, this was an edgy concept. This time there was no channel conflict! We ambitiously launched a national race series with a party after each race. The idea is to engage the consumer by giving them an extended experience in our products. This creates an emotional tie to our company, and gives the consumer a reason to buy more of our products and attend our events again. It was met with HUGE excitement and a massive influx of press.

Are there any ways that you have leveraged the Internet to grow your business?

Our core business is built around the Internet, and our Website is our best marketing tool. We also have a grassroots program we call the Skirt Entourage. These are 20+ women (aged 30–55) who are fanatical about SkirtSports. They post blog and message board entries all over the place. We also partner with other companies who have online databases to promote our business.

What challenges have you faced and how have you overcome them?

Personnel issues are some of the toughest. I grow emotionally attached to my employees and it is tough when things don't work out.

If you were starting over today, what would you do differently?

- I would not spend more money than we have!
- I would learn the actual time lines of our industry and stick to them.
- I would not give away so much product.
- I would let people go as soon as I knew they were not working out instead of lingering....
- I would be tougher with my standards and demand the quality and service that I paid for.

What advice do you have for other business owners?

Develop your own board of advisors immediately and call on them often. Encourage your employees to develop their own board of advisors, too. Everyone needs input. Do not micromanage. The best management is allowing people to manage themselves. Ask a TON of questions. Everything takes longer and costs more than you think. If you don't take care of yourself, it will come back to haunt you.

CHAPTER 14

"Leadership and learning are indispensable to each other."

—John F. Kennedy

Always Be Learning

95 Be a Reader

A funny thing happened on the way to writing this book. I surveyed and interviewed dozens of business owners. One of the questions I asked was, "Are there any books that you recommend?" I was pleasantly surprised that the vast majority said something like, "Oh, there are so many." Clearly, successful business owners have one thing in common: they're reading.

Here are the top books that were repeatedly cited during interviews. Many of these authors also took time to contribute their advice for this book, and I am grateful for that.

The E-Myth Revisited: Why Most Small Businesses Don't Work and What to Do About It by Michael Gerber

The New Rules of Marketing and PR: How to Use News Releases, Blogs, Podcasting, Viral Marketing and Online Media to Reach Buyers Directly by David Meerman Scott

Getting Things Done: The Art of Stress-Free Productivity by David Allen

Good to Great: Why Some Companies Make the Leap and Others Don't by Jim Collins

Meatball Sundae: Is Your Marketing Out of Sync? by Seth Godin

Nice Girls DO Get the Sale: Relationship-Building that Gets Results by Elinor Stutz

Blue Ocean Strategy: How to Create Uncontested Market Space and Make Competition Irrelevant by W. Chan Kim and Renée Mauborgne

Million Dollar Consulting: The Professional's Guide to Growing a Practice by Alan Weiss

Rain Making: Attract New Clients No Matter What Your Field by Ford Harding

Built to Last: Successful Habits of Visionary Companies by Jim Collins and Jerry I. Porras

Bonus: A downloadable reading list with all of the books referenced in this book is available at *www.BusinessInfoGuide.com/leap-downloads.*

96 Build Your Mobile Classroom

I bought an iPod specifically so that I could listen to business audios: teleseminars, audio books, podcasts, and so forth. I have turned my car into a mobile classroom by always having a book or something interesting playing. It does wonders for removing the pain out of long drives and traffic.

If you're one of those people who believes that you don't have the attention span for audios, I have two pieces of advice for you:

1. You need to find a great book with an equally great narrator so that you have no choice but to get hooked. I love it when the author reads the book. Try anything by Michael Gerber or Seth Godin.

2. Listening is a skill. Keep trying until you get hooked. Trust me: it's worth it.

For downloadable audio books, check out *www.audible.com.* Personal development systems on audio are available at *www.nightingale.com/.*

97 Attend Classes and Seminars

With classes at your local colleges and adult learning centers, there are abundant opportunities to learn new skills. If you struggle with the Internet, take a class. Want to learn how to analyze your financial statements? Take a class.

Seminars and classes through trade organizations also provide a wonderful learning opportunity. Every time I attend a weekend-long or even week-long event, I leave energized. Between learning new skills, meeting new people, and being exposed to a new environment, you just can't go wrong by participating in seminars with trade associations related to your industry.

In fact, I challenge you to attend at least one each year—or two if you're really ambitious. If you look in the right places, you will find value in attending and should make some interesting friends along the way.

98 Read Industry Publications

I visited a client once who pointed at a stack of newsletters on his desk. "They're from all the organizations I belong to," he told me. "I know I should read them, but I just never have enough time." Can you relate?

Here's the deal: At the very least, skim through them. If there is a valuable nugget in there (and there probably is), then you will be glad you did. We live in an extremely fast-paced world. Blink and you will miss something big. You owe it to yourself and your customers to stay on top of trends in your industry and to always look for ways to improve. If you are constantly learning and improving, you will have no place to go but up.

Whether print newsletters, electronic newsletters, blogs, or message boards, don't lose track of what's happening in your industry. That same client, the one who didn't want to read his newsletters, was also averse to technology. He said, "I know I should be on board with it, but it's just one more thing on a long list of things I need to do." I guarantee you his business is going to suffer as a result. Perhaps if he were opening the newsletters, he would understand the important advances happening in his industry.

99 Learn From Mistakes

I don't know anyone in business who hasn't made a mistake. That is the beauty of life. It's like watching babies learn to walk. They fall down and get up again. Sometimes they get frustrated and cry. But they keep trying and learn lessons like "don't try to step over the cat."

Maybe it's all the Wayne Dyer programs I've listened to, but I am always looking for the lesson. Bad things happen, things don't go as planned, and the unexpected makes an appearance. Some of my best lessons have come from taking a wrong turn. Here are a few:

- Don't waste money on an office unless you're going to use it.

- When you own a retail store and place an ad offering something for free, people are going to show up—all the wrong kinds of people.

- Speaking to groups that don't represent my target audience is not a good use of my time.

- Social networking can turn into a time-waster if I'm not careful. Designate a start and stop time in my schedule.

- Don't rely on one piece of technology. Have a backup.

When something goes wrong, after I recover from my initial reaction, I look for the lesson. One of my friends, Hal Elrod, an author and motivational speaker with an incredible life story (*www.YoPalHal.com*)—he was hit head-on by a drunk driver and pronounced dead on the scene, and went on to a long recovery with short-term memory loss due to the injury to his brain—sent me an e-mail on my birthday last year with a thoughtful message:

> *"Remember, you are exactly where you are*
> *supposed to be in your life right now."*

This is a reminder that things happen for a reason. Maybe you didn't land that big account you wanted. Maybe you invested money in a promise that didn't deliver. Whatever happens, look for the lesson and you will uncover the hidden magic. Because you are exactly where you are supposed to be right now.

100 Capture and Cultivate Ideas

One of my most treasured business development tools is an 8x11 hardbound spiral notebook. My "idea journal" is where all of my business ideas are logged. It's a place to get them out of my head and on to paper, and a place for brainstorming.

Most entrepreneurs have no shortage of ideas. I have found that keeping them in one place is a great way to let them "simmer" while I flesh out the details. I have also found that it's often better to let ideas bake for a while before jumping in to launch them. Sometimes an idea that seems brilliant at 2:00 a.m. looks completely different in the light of day.

To get the most from your own idea journal, get in the habit of jotting everything down—from simple marketing ideas to major business changes. Then schedule some quiet time to tap into your creativity and wisdom with a good brainstorming session. When things get too busy, you can always return to your journal later, knowing that you've captured your most important thoughts.

101 Just *LEAP*

The fact that you are an entrepreneur means that you are a risk-taker. There's no way around it. It's what we do. But some take more risks than others, and in my experience, the right risk can lead to big rewards.

You take a risk when you launch a new product or service, test a new marketing campaign, hire an employee, invest in technology, take out a loan, submit a post on your blog, or send a tweet through Twitter, and during all kinds of random business scenarios.

Many of the risks I have taken have paid off. Each book I have written has come with its own rewards. I have built and sold a business. I have launched new business ventures. I have opened up with a mastermind group. I have learned some lessons the hard way and as long as I don't repeat them, the lessons are almost always worthwhile.

Take risks. *LEAP! The secret is to never bet more than you can afford to lose.* Take calculated risks and enjoy the rewards. Oh, and remember to enjoy the ride!

Index

About the Author

STEPHANIE CHANDLER is an author of several business and marketing books, including *The Author's Guide to Building an Online Platform: Leveraging the Internet to Sell More Books* and *From Entrepreneur to Infopreneur: Make Money with Books, eBooks and Information Products.* She is also founder and CEO of Authority Publishing (*www.AuthorityPublishing.com*), which provides custom book publishing and author marketing services for business, self-help, and other non-fiction books, and BusinessInfoGuide.com, a directory of resources for entrepreneurs.

A frequent speaker at business events and on the radio, Stephanie has been featured in *Entrepreneur Magazine, BusinessWeek, Inc.com, MORE Magazine,* and many other media outlets. For author and speaker details, visit *www.StephanieChandler.com.*

Stephanie resides near Sacramento, California, with her husband, teenage stepson, and 3-year-old son. She loves to escape for weekends in Lake Tahoe and any vacation that involves tropical scenery, a beach chair, and a good book, and she is a supporter of several animal-rescue organizations.